Other titles
by
Corey Hamilton

Keep Left
Society's Grip
Exit Is A Safe Place
Open Up
Mash Notes
Mash Notes: vol 2
Too Personal
Lonely Night Songs
2 Days
Unhyped
Time Marches On
Thirty Three
VI
What If?
Magic Bus
How I Remember It
Cease & Desist
Sensible Shoes
Do Not Ever Have Any Good Ideas
DNA
I Am NOT With The Band
Wedge Politics
My Side Project

NO one

shall BE spaRED

Copyright © 2003 Corey Hamilton

All rights reserved. No part of this book may be reproduced or transmitted in any form or by any means, graphic, mechanical or electronic, including photocopying and recording, or by any information storage or retrieval system without written permission from the publisher, except for brief passages quoted in review.

Library and Archives Canada Cataloguing in Publication

Hamilton, Coery, 1971-
   No one shall be spared / Corey Hamilton.

Poems and prose.
ISBN 978-0-9697305-3-8

   I. Title.

PS8565.A5347N6 2008   C811'.54   C2007-906817-0

All photography © 2003 by Corey Hamilton except author photographs on final page © 2008 by Randall Edwards/www.redwardsphoto.com
Design/Layout by Corey Hamilton

First Printing

Published by Dramatic Situations
         P.O. Box 696
         Edmonton, AB
         T5J 2L4
         CANADA
www.dramaticsituations.com

NO

shall BE

> "An artist's only concern is to shoot for some kind of perfection, and *on his own terms*, not anyone else's."
>
> "Franny and Zooey"
> J.D. Salinger

#1265

thANK$

thaNK$ tO alL oF tHE bulliE$ iN sCHoOl, woRK & eVERywHEre eLe, THi goE$ oUT TO YOu aLl. ThaNK$ tO aLL oF tHE $trANGer$, aCQaINtXXXANCE$, frienD$, loVER$ aND faMILy wHO diXXdN'T CARe aBOut mY wOrk aNd $HouID hAVe, tHI$ defiNITELy gOEs Out tO aLL oF yoU. tHANK$ tO aLl of tHe frIEndS$ ANd 1over$ wHO baILeD oN mE, tHI$ of cOUr$e gOEs oUt tO yoU. tHAnk$ tO aLL of thE MEDia, artIt, cRItI¢$, puBLi$hER$ aND gaLLerIE$ wHO sAId mY wOrk Wa$ tOO mUch oF oNE tHIng aNd nOT eNOugh of aNOTHEr. THI$ fuCK yoU goE$$ ouT tO yoU. YOuaLL mAdE mE wHAt i aM todAY. thANK$. i hOPe tHAt yOU aRE prouD oF mE aNd MY wOrk.

$IN¢erE tHAnk$ tO tHe $elE¢T, ¢Hoi¢e fEW wHO $uPPORTeD mE wHOlehEArtED1Y, evEN iF thEy dIDn'T agrEE wiTH mE aLL oXf tHE tIMe. yOU kEEp mE goiNG thrOUCh tHE dARk tIME$. $IN¢erE 1OVE gOE$ oUT tO tHE$e fEW, YoU kNOw wHo YOu Are. thAnk$.

It is also the job of the artist to police himself, NOT others policing the artist, contrary to popular belief.

tHANK$ aXgaiN!

COREY HAMILTON

#1152

NO ONE SHALL BE SPARED

What you are about to read
Is not pure fiction
What you are about to read
Is not purely coincidence
The people, places and events inside
Are all real
What you are about to read
Is the truth
The whole truth
And nothing but the truth
So help your god
This is not a monopoly
Or rather
By the end of this
It will be a monopoly
Because my use of negative space
Is the best in the land
But I am not doing this
To be cool
But given the chance
I would probably sell out
This is sexist
This is narrow minded
This is xenophobic
This is bigoted
This is kick you out
Before you finish your meal
This is shoot you in the face
After I have given you
Your two weeks notice
This <u>IS</u> anger management
This is offensive
I am offensive
This is opinionated
I am opinionated
This is a breach of trust
<u>YOU</u> are a breach of trust
This is burning your house down
While you are snuggled up

In your bed late at night
This is the hole in the ozone layer
I am the hole in the ozone layer
This is bloody vomit on your suburban sidewalk
I am bloody vomit on your suburban sidewalk
This is splitting your world in pieces
And this has just started
But by the end of this
You will ask me
How did I end up this way
And I will ask you
Why did you push me to end up this way
And I will think
I don't like being this way
But when you are polarized
Sometimes you regret things
Regret is regrettable
This is the truth
The whole truth
And nothing but the truth
So help your god
This is me
And you gave birth to me
Because I am a product of your system
And now I have come
To show you what you have created
With your sexist, narrow minded, bigoted, xenophobic Renaissance
Now I don't give you two weeks notice
I just show up in your office bright and early in the morning
And show you
Your family's bloody, decapitated heads
In a black garbage bag
This is a loud diatribe
A rant
At three in the morning
On a week night
This is a last warning
Before the bombs drops
This is can't put down pages
Because you put me down
On these pages

If you aren't offended
By what you are about to read
Then you are part of the problem
So don't be surprised
When it blows up in your face
This is your last warning
O.K.
Read 'em an' weep
You've been warned
This is my personal disclaimer to you
Fucker.

FOR WINDOWS

#948

-SET THE TABLE-

    This was written ages ago.
    This was chipped into stone by elders.
    This was carved into wood by medicine men.
    This was written on parchment long before your saviour was even conceived.
    This was typed down in the morning before your first coffee.
    This is spray painted graffiti done on walls under cover of darkness.
    This is saved archivally on all of your discs, cds and hard drives.
    And when you turn it up, open it up, decipher it, you will regret every second of your miserable life.
    And when you are at your lowest point I will come to tell you that you are of no use to anyone anymore and that you must live another thousand years for your crimes. I will tell you the secrets of despair.

FOR I AM THE KING OF MY DESPAIR AND YOUR HATRED.

-BRING THE FOOD-

He didn't even get a chance to breathe.
She didn't even have a name yet.
Because you fucked around so much and it cost everyone around you as well as yourself. That's what you get for "just screwing around." It ends up not being true and/or real and you end up looking like a fake. Your work looks worse than you, but what do you know, you never had an anthem in your life. You are a waste of human potential.

Banshee.
That's what I thought when I remembered a dream I had about a co-worker. In the dream her lover and her were constantly changing shape to hide the fact that they were gay. They would change into owls, wolves and the sort to hide their baby. Thinking about them made me happy. Thinking about your restrictions on them made me want to puke. I wish that they could scream about their love without having a half full beer bottle thrown at their heads. Fuck you and your restrictions. I hope that you get a baseball bat in your ass and a broom handle in your throat for your bullshit that you put them and others like them through.
That's why I thought banshee.

I was watching television the other night and I saw a story that made my stomach upset. It was a story about some useless white jock trash, at a school in the U.S., that raped a girl with a broom handle and a baseball bat. The girl happened to be mentally challenged.
When I found out that the story was true, I couldn't watch anymore. The boys who did this should have their penises and all other appendages amputated. Luckily the girl won't turn out to be a bitter bitch who persecutes me for having a dick, because she has a good family and good friends to keep her on track. Some women aren't so lucky and turn out to be bitter bitches and/or get depressed and/or kill themselves.
But now I am getting off topic, I just want to be left alone with those assholes so I can take out my anger on boys who ruin women's lives like that, and inadvertently ruin mine.
Just give me an hour.
Just give me a chainsaw.
And I will show them real power.

...the boys I mean...

I changed pens a little while ago, but that doesn't mean I am going to get abstract on your ass just yet. If you want abstract right now then go eat Picasso's shit up. Because abstract isn't in for me. More of that later.

On Tuesday May 4th, 1999 my long time psychologist died of an apparent heart attack. About a year ago he had to quit his job because of the stress. So I had to see someone new.
I just found out that he died a little while ago at work. I thought I could handle work, but I just got tired out thinking that someone like him has to die when that piece of trash woman who molested me for years will probably out live me.
People like her are lucky I don't have a gun.

I knew you would stick around those others instead of me. It doesn't piss me off though, because it just means one less weakling to deal with.

I have an open wound on my foot, that when I spread my toes in balance or in pleasure it shoots pain into my foot. This wound reminds me of you, my first girlfriend, because every time I see the wound, I want to slit it open wider with a razor blade to make it worse. Making it worse reminds me of how you used to treat me and how you dumped me. I am glad I hung up on you the last time we talked on the phone, or ever for that fact, because you are just a spineless bitch that could never deal with me. You are such a typical bitch woman.

Misogyny landscape because of you and the likes of you bitch. You tainted my view of the stronger sex because you are a weak bitch. I hope your next boyfriend treats you the way you treated me, and makes you dislike, no hate men. Eye for an eye bitch.

You know where "it's" at?! Yeah, right. You wouldn't know where "it's" at if I put "it" on a pitchfork and hit you in the chest with "it".

I have been pondering a few things. Like, why is it when a woman says she wants to cut a man's penis off with a machete, it's empowering and when a man says he wants to take a machete to a woman's vagina, he should be charged with sexual harassment?

Or, how about this...how come when a man sleeps around he's a stud and when a woman sleeps around she's a slut?

You wouldn't give either examples a second thought would you? Even the white trash rebelling from their suburban history by wearing dreadlocks, getting facial piercings and smoking lots of dope and cigarettes and drinking lots of coffee and alcohol would skirt these queries.

Double standards you weak piece of shit.

It's strange how my mind works. I see your pretty face sometimes on my way to work in the morning and sometimes you say hello. It's strange how my mind works because I want you to be so much more to me but I know it won't happen because I am too scared to talk to you and we still live in a male dominated society, so you can't approach me. I hold nothing against you because if you were to approach me there is a chance I could be a typical pig male and think you want to have sex with me. Or maybe your friends would give you shit. I don't know. I do know that I almost want you to deal with me the same way your co-worker does...ignore me or sigh and look at the ceiling and walk away. It's strange how my mind works.

Respect is a rare commodity.

I have lost all hope for humanity.

This has come about because of my interaction with people in my job. Most of the people I meet are morons and it surprises me that they can get dressed by themselves in the morning...or even breathe for that fact.

I have seen trend with people. Most single women over 40 are bitchy morons. Most single men over forty are desperate bitter morons. Men who have toothpicks in their mouths are asshole morons. Most East Indian and Chinese people always want deals. Most retired people are in a rush. Most young people, who are under 30, are not in a rush. I can't figure any of this out. I have discussed this with my co-workers (some of whom fall into these categories and don't follow these mosts) agree with most of this.

The more people I meet, the more I realize why there are wars and racism and few people willing to work in retail.

Victim.

You always play the victim just because your parents are divorced. You always play the victim because you are from a single parent household. Or you always play the victim because you have a disease that may kill you.

Why is it that people who have divorced parents, or come from a single parent household have so many issues? I know one person with divorced parents who is cool with it. The rest of you play the victim. As for you, I have little respect for you with your disease because you are a jerk to everyone because you have this disease and everyone around you doesn't. I have met people who have A.I.D.S. who don't play the victim, maybe because it was brought out because of their own stupidity...so that may not be a fair comparison, but the A.I.D.S. people I have met don't play the victim. Regardless, I have respect for them and not any of you.

Victim.

But you insist on being a miserable when your ailment is out of your hands.

But you insist on being miserable when your parents' divorce is out of your hands.

I lump you people together because you all play the victim and you are all miserable. So you make everyone else's lives miserable too.

Everyone's a victim.

It's just that some people move on. If you can't move on then go home and never leave home or kill yourself. Both are viable options in my eyes. Just because you are miserable doesn't mean everyone else should be too. Some people actually have a good life. If you can't handle that some people have good lives then use one of my two options, or better yet, use both. Make room for people who want to enjoy life.

Victim.

I hate that word.

If the Reform Party (update: it's now the Canadian Alliance...er...P.C.s...er...whatever) gets into power I will buy a bunch of guns, hate gays and North American Aboriginals, shout obscenities at people on the street with alternative lifestyles, all from the comfort of my newly bought monster truck. Well, no I won't, because it's unoriginal because it's already being done by right wing nazis all over the nation.

What I would really do is move...to another planet.

Common sense is a rare commodity.

I manifest banding in the shadow areas because I feel we shouldn't let another immigrant inside Canada until we solve our own problems. Like unemployment, inflation, low Canadian dollar, aboriginal rights, homeless people, the Quebec separation issue, etc., etc., etc.. Letting more people in to leech off of Canada's positives while some Canadians can't even take advantage of some of these positives. The more people we let in, the more cooks ruin the meal.

Why is it that all of the lesbians I meet are bitter and/or screwed in the head? Why is it that all of the bisexuals I meet are absolute flakes? Maybe I am the enemy to lesbians, I don't know. I do know that I have never ever had a problem with a homosexual man. I mean I am overweight and of average looks and intelligence so I can't see them wanting to just get in my pants. Lesbians? Get your heads out of your asses. Just because I am not gay doesn't mean I deserve to be disrespected. Remember, disrespect is a two way street. What goes around comes around bitches. But I guess you may think the same about artists like me. I guess everything is relative.

I just wrote a bunch of cheques out with this very pen and not one was made out to you. The names on the cheques earned my money. You don't deserve a cent from me so go fuck yourself.

Let Quebec separate, but don't give them anything from the rest of Canada. They don't deserve anything if they separate. They have to try and make it on their own. What I am willing to do is give them 3 months before they start whining about how tough they have it...again. I am also willing to start taking bets on when the whining from Quebec will start again. Like, if it will be sooner than 3 months after they separate or later. Let them separate, I want to laugh at them when Quebec goes broke (if it isn't already) and say, "I told you so."

My true colors are as bright as my art, my body and my body art.

This is anger management.

I am now going to be called a misogynist. I am now going to be called a bigot, a racist, a homophobe and a xenophobe. People will now say that discrimination is part of my profile. I am writing this late at night. This is the only reason I am up late, otherwise I would and soon will, sleep like a baby.

I work with a polish lady, a german lady, a half black teenager, a Sri Lankan lady and my best friend is Chilean.

I am not bragging.

All of what I write about are facts. If you don't like it, then there's the door. Use it. I don't have to justify what I say because it's what I know and feel. If you don't like it, then burn it. For I don't need you on my ship. So piss off. I will now sleep like a baby.

Look, there's a paradox ahead.

Last summer, as usual, I shaved my head. I went into work wearing a golf shirt. People stare and make comments but I am pretty much used to it. An extremely overweight man came in and I quickly realized that he was a moronic asshole, for after I politely served him he said "I didn't know that they gave jobs to people like you." He then left. The Sri Lankan lady I work with had at least two incidents of ignorance and disrespect aimed at her.

The first: A couple came in to buy the same camera for the fourth time. Three times before they would buy the camera and return it within two weeks and get a refund, as per policy. This time it was the Sri Lankan lady serving them and coincidentally enough the couple was also Sri Lankan. They said that they would use it for their friend's wedding and return for a refund in a few days. They did all of this in Sri Lankan. My Sri Lankan co-worker played dumb and when they said they would buy it she asked them several times if they were happy with their purchase, and every time they said, yes, they were happy with their purchase. So my co-worker rang up the sale but put a note on the receipt which said "under no circumstances may this camera be returned. this sale is final." The couple were extremely flustered when they read the note and said that they though that there was a two week full refund policy. My co-worker countered by saying that "you obviously like the camera because you purchased it three times before." They spoke in Sri Lankan to each other, with the husband saying "now what are we going to do?" My Sri Lankan co-worker let them stew a bit and finally the pair left.

My Sri Lankan co-worker and I agree that it is the height of rudeness to converse in a foreign language in front of someone who doesn't understand. So it serves the couple right for getting busted.

Now I see what sort of games you people play when you are talking your shit, it's just a chicken shit way of being an asshole to me. I have no respect for you whatsoever.but I do have a millimeter more respect for the overweight moronic asshole I spoke of earlier because he had the guts to say it to my face.You are too chicken shit to say your bullshit to my face. Now do you see why I won't even smile at you. Fuck you.

The second: A white redneck looking farmer was dealing with my Sri Lankan co-worker but wasn't paying much attention to her. Suddenly, he started smiling and in a low voice said, "What's a black bitch like you working in a white place like this?" My co-worker asked him to leave and he did.

You fucking piece of shit, if I was near you, I would have busted your head open. At least I can grow my hair out and cover my tattoos with a long sleeved shirt. My co-worker is stuck in your narrow minded world. I hate your fucking guts.

Sometimes I only like myself, my family, my small circle of friends and a few of my co-workers.

You never even considered me. How considerate of you. All of it done in front of me. How considerate of you. I hope everything doesn't work out for you in the end. That will be my gift to you. How considerate of me, how considerate of you.

Every day I work I hear and see disrespectful children screaming or crying. If I ever pulled that as a child I would have been taken outside and smacked and never brought out in public again. I would have deserved it all. It would have taught me respect, something that a lot of parents don't do now a days.

So it was quite a contrast for me when I sat and chatted with an eight year old boy for the better part of an hour. I would have been proud to be the father of such a mature and respectful child. We need more children like that young boy.

Your father sent me to kill you.

Unrepentant.

I have to get to that kid early because I am not ambidextrous and when push comes to shove, I will shoot that kid in the face.

Unrepentant

What you did, is a compliment to me. What you didn't do, is an insult to me.

Unrepentant.

What you will do will bring me to be flattered and what you won't do will repulse me.

Unrepentant.

You are that kid and when you die at my hands I will laugh at your family and friends.

Unrepentant.
Unrepentant.

When I see a beautiful woman getting drunk and/or smoking and/or doing drugs I am suddenly repulsed to the point of being sick to my stomach.

You make me feel as if I am the dead in deadline. You make me feel as if I am what the cat dragged in. You make me feel as if I am on the thirteenth floor and I can't go anywhere without ducking under a ladder, walking on the remnants of broken mirrors and black cats are always crossing my path. You make me feel as if I should apologize for having a penis. I resent your treatment of me, and the only reason I ignore you is because I work with you. You are a disrespectful child. I will wait and hide in the weeds until my anger grows too big to hide, and then, and only then, I will lash out at you. Scarring you, until you finally learn to grow up.

Epoch.

I smear my blood over my bed sheets and go to sleep in it. I had nothing better to do last night, for you never invited me. Probably because I am too straight for you. Probably because I don't drink alcohol or do drugs or smoke cigarettes. Probably because I am a loner too. I will remember that.

I will remember.

For I remember everything. There won't be any compromising. For I will remember everything.

I will remember.

I remember everything. Whether I like to or not, I remember everything. I am totally indifferent to my memory because sometimes it is a good attribute and sometimes it is a downright nasty one. It all evens out. Sometimes I remember the beautiful morning walks with my Grandfather, and sometimes I remember the time that that woman molested me. I remember these memories as clearly as I see my writing on this paper. I have seen a higher purpose for my memory. I sometimes believe that when you betray me, ridicule me, knock me down or burn me that you will get your's. It's a sometimes belief because although what I see, hear and feel I will always remember I sometimes won't see you get your's. So as the saying goes, out of sight, out of mind. So all I can do is hope that you get your's and whether I do or don't see, hear, feel you get yours, just the hope that you will get yours puts a smile on my face. Next to my creations, the biggest joy in my life is one of my memories coming back to haunt you, and when it does, I will smile, shake my head and say under my breath that it couldn't have happened to a better person. I will remember that too. I will remember.

I <u>will</u> remember.

Epoch.

Most aboriginals who I worked with and came in to where I worked were extremely nice (I have to try and ignore the surly drunk ones begging for change on the street though), even though in some of their eyes I am the enemy. The one incident that sticks in my memory that happened at work was different. An aboriginal couple reeking of alcohol came in to look at cameras. I showed them a couple and they settled on the first one, so I rang up the sale and told them the price including G.S.T.. They said that because they live on the reserve they don't have to pay the G.S.T..I informed them that they weren't on the reserve and maybe they should buy it on the reserve. They responded by saying that they don't have cameras on the reserve. I stood silent at first and then asked if they would still like to purchase the camera. The man's response was, "No. Go fuck yourself racist." They then left. Maybe I could have handled that one better? I don't know.

No one is safe here. If you have wronged, you will now pay.

Ever since I was publicly called an iconoclast, you have not come into where I work.

The heat is stifling, it makes me want to murder.
Help! I've been Johned and I can't get up!

Who runs your show?

A bigot.

Jew parents disowning their offspring for not marrying another jew.

A bigot.

White parents disowning their offspring for marrying a "colored" person.

A bigot.

Black parents disowning their offspring for not marrying another black person.

A bigot.

Narrow minded bigots who should be buried alive in a fire ants den.

A bigot.

Sure as shit stinks all the half black and half white women I meet have attitude problems and all of the half black and half white men I meet <u>don't</u> have attitude problems.

Sure as shit stinks.

I hear so many immigrants (new and old) complaining about Canada. If you don't like it then go back where you came from. Go on! You are not wanted here so go! You have it easy here. Just because things don't go your way you bitch. Fuck you. Go back, but you don't want to because you left a negative situation or something, I don't know and I don't care. So when things don't go your way you complain. Go back! Turbans in the R.C.M.P., fuck you! Why should we change for you? If we moved to your country we would be treated worse than shit. So quit your bitching or go back where you came from...or better yet, both.

The Sri Lankan lady I work with was telling me how some of her Sri Lankan friends were complaining how hard it is in Canada. Saying that life in Sri Lanka was easier, they had maids and such. My co-worker offered to buy them a one way ticket back to Sri Lanka. They never complained to her again.

Years ago I cut out a letter to the editor in a local newspaper. It was an extremely well written letter saying that new and old immigrants who complained about Canada and wanted Canada to change for them were giving a bad name to all the respectful immigrants and that they should accept Canada for what it is because it is a lot better than what they left behind. The letter was written by an East Indian immigrant. I melt this all together because I know that I will be called a racist. I hope that these pieces will lessen the blows against me. In my peace, at least I know that there are at least two immigrants who agree with me. I will sleep easy with a smile on my face tonight.

I know what you look like. Cramped down in your corner and when you answer to me you will die instantly. I know what you look like.

First rape conviction gets 10 years in prison and counselling. Second rape conviction, the death penalty. Simple as that. If you have to get your power trip by abusing and/or at the expense of someone else then you don't deserve to live. Simple as that. Same thing goes for child molesters. Simple as that. Simple as that.

I don't want to get evicted, but I demand respect from you. I will respect you for being brave in coming from somewhere else to here because you are taking a big chance. But that doesn't give you the right to disrespect me because my culture (or lack there of) is so different. I demand respect from you or else I will shoot you in the face every time I see you. If you disrespect me then this is what I will do, or at the very least I will disrespect you. If you don't like it here, then go back where you came from.

And I don't even own a gun.
And I don't even own a gun?

Epoch.

Quebecois and Albertan separatists are paralyzed from the neck up.

I am such an asshole now.

Epoch.

I am having to move to a new apartment I live in a dive and he is raising the rent.
Again.

Epoch.

Fuck him if he thinks I am going to pay one cent more for a shitty bachelor that has shitty security and is surrounded by a bunch of mindless, religious buttfucks who give me static every time they see me go to my car.

Epoch.

I hope that this piece of shit building burns to the ground the second after I leave it for the last time.

Epoch.

Epoch.

As long as my mind is active, I don't care about my body.
Epoch.

I am now moving somewhere else in this city. I will give everything a little more time and then I will find a new city.
Epoch.

If you saw me now you wouldn't recognize me. If you think I look different now, just wait until after I give everything a little more time. Your recognition of me disappears and I couldn't give a fuck.
Epoch.

Mark this day on your calendar because it's the day I stop caring about you and your insecure bullshit and start caring even more about my work. Fuck you and your mindless, pompous, insecure, verbose ramblings. What little respect I had for you went down the toilet when I noticed that you couldn't even sign your name.

Epoch.

As long as my mind is active I will keep moving so your recognition of me disappears and my work carries me on and on and on and fuck you and your mindless, pompous, insecure, verbose ramblings about me because it is much too late for apologies. Fuck you. Mark this day on your calendar because in no time at all I will break into your home in broad daylight and put a bullet in your already rotting skull.

Epoch.

Fuck you.

Epoch.

<u>Epoch.</u>

-EAT THE MEAL-

Tread lightly on public land.

Tread lightly on public land?

Tread lightly on public land?! Fuck you and people like you who "just screw around" and never tread lightly on my land, so why should I tread lightly on yours? Fuck you, tread lightly on public land, yeah right. One shit turn deserves another.

All the banshees screaming wake me up at night. I don't mince words anymore because I got the feeling that your attitudes have got to change or myself or someone like myself is going to bury you alive in a hole. You can't apologize for your actions and/or attitudes because while you bury your head in the sand we will push you in deeper until you die. Then we will forget about you and go to sleep with smiles on our faces and never wake up in the middle of the night again.

If I had my way, the whole lot of you would be dead. Men who rape and talk sexist drivel and women who persecute me for having a dick and talk your sexist drivel. You are all the same, whether you step forward or back, you step on me. I have no idea why you all do this. That is why I have ill feelings toward you all.

Death to abstractions.

The lights are very bright in here. It is punishment for not going to his funeral. I will atone for it by not going to her funeral.

I keep on giving out and getting nothing in return. I guess...it's just one less weakling to deal with.

Judas.
You typical bitch woman. When you read this you will be shot in the face. Right after you finish reading this...you will die.

Judas.

This came from the future to kill your children, this came from the past to kill you and this has come from the present to kill me.

Eye for an eye.
Do you even notice this bitch? I am just banging on a piano just to make noise just so I don't hear my misogynistic landscape that your misandry vomit helped create. I am tired of your misandry bullshit bitch. You are not even second place. Second place is the first loser bitch, and you are so weak that you dropped out of the top ten. You are weak and you have got another thing coming. It will hit you between your eyes, knocking you flat on your back, knocking the wind out of you, knocking you up with a rabies filled child and the whole mess will stun you into submission. I don't even know how to play piano. I just bang on it to drown out all of our past conversations that I remember. Do you even notice this bitch? I hope that you get burned just like the way you burned me.
Eye for an eye bitch.

You still don't know where it's at because I burned every bridge after I crossed them and I have no remorse or regret.

Rare commodity is a respect.

It's strange how my mind works. It's like a trap. I want you more when you are far away and if you come close I seem to push you away. I fear nothing but myself. I have prepared for this. You shall all die and I won't shed a tear. So stay far away.

I have lost all hope for humanity. You are all no better than a cow or a moose...or even a rock.

Death to racists, nazis, the K.K.K. and all other fucking idiots like them. I need another planet to move to.

There are so many cooks that the meal has been burned to a crispy pulp.

Rare commodity is a common sense.

Not one person slept last night. Even the people in beds miles and days away could see my arc light of colors. I hope it burns everyone's retinas.

I told you once already and I won't tell you again you fucking post...this <u>IS</u> anger management.

This is not a syllogism. It's one way coming from me to you. My laughter changed to sobbing. My thoughts of staying home ended up changing to thoughts of moving to somewhere that i would be recognized less, if at all.

I am going to be called everything negative in the book. In this or that book too. I will still sleep like a baby.

You are still discriminating towards my dark skinned co-worker and even me for having small things like a bald head and tattoos. Go talk your chicken shit language that I don't understand somewhere else you piece of shit. Fuck you.

Sometimes I only like myself and my small circle of friends and a few co-workers.

I left out my family.

I left out my family because they don't respect me. Or at least it seems that way. Or at least they have a strange way of showing respect. But then again, so do I. But then again I am worse than my family sometimes. Sometimes. Don't you tell me otherwise because it has seemed that way for years.

It is time for me to walk away.

It is time for me to walk away from the racist and/or disrespectful people,walk away from the racist and disrespectful people.Fuck the whole lot of you pieces of shit.

The family and a couple of friends I let go of most of the time because they have stood by me, so I respect them. But I still hold grudges. I wish I could let go totally.

It is time for me to walk away.

It is time for me to walk away from the racist and/or disrespectful people, walk away from the racist and disrespectful people. Fuck the whole lot of you pieces of shit.

Look out! You're going to hit the paradox!

You never even considered me. How considerate of you. You don't know that I never said anything. You see me as a novelty. When everything goes wrong for you I will wear a smile constantly for the next month and a half. This will be my gift to you. How considerate of me. How considerate of you.

I was taught respect as a child. You should do the same with your children or they will never grow up. Why yes...I am telling you how to be a parent. Someone has to because it is quite obvious that you need some help.

Were you taught respect as a child?
I was.
It was the high point of my life.

It is not my concern as to why it is that he wants you killed. Your father has sent me to kill you and it shall be done because he paid me good money to do it. Fuck you, get ready to die.

Unrepentant

Ninety days after I was born you murdered me, but because they bury the dead so quickly I was never given the chance. Not soon enough for some people but for others, I should have been left out for months.

Unrepentant.

I will wait in the weeds silently watching you fuck me over. And when it all comes back to bite you in the ass I will just go home to sleep with a smile on my face.

Unrepentant.

I will eventually get my revenge, and when I do, you will die instantly at the hands of my work.

Unrepentant.

<u>Unrepentant.</u>

Hello. Nice to meet you. Is that a cigarette, and are you drunk? You are? Goodbye.

I won't waste my time with a woman who intentionally destroys her body (not to mention mind). No matter how intelligent or beautiful she is. I won't waste my time with <u>anyone</u> who intentionally destroys their body (not to mention mind) for that fact.

I lashed out at you for being a disrespectful, petulant child and you are still the same disrespectful, petulant child. I won't apologize for who I am and what I stand for and I especially won't apologize for my physical attributes. Fuck you. I hope that your worst nightmare comes true.

Fuck you.

<u>Epoch.</u>

I had dug my heels in but now I come out of the weeds for the first and last time. Smeared with my own blood and I will remember it all. I remember getting brushed off by you. I remember getting ridiculed by you. I remember getting molested by you. I remember getting beaten by you. And last but not least, I remember getting murdered by you. I was left in a ditch off of the side of a dusty road with the noise of the passing apathetic traffic as my funeral march/music. It is now coming back to kick you in the knees. I am now smiling, shaking my head and saying under my breath that it couldn't have happened to a nicer per-

son. I remember what you did to me and I will remember how it all came back to haunt you and then murder you.
I will remember.
I remember.

Epoch!

No one is safe here. If you have wronged, then payment is due.

Even if it is true that I <u>am</u> an iconoclast, it doesn't mean we can't associate with each other. Does it?

The murder is stifling. It makes me want to heat.
Help! I've been Johned and I can't even get it up!

This is the last time I will ask you before I use a drill with a one inch drill bit to drill a hole in each of your knee caps, <u>who runs your show?!</u> I run my own, do you run your own?

At least <u>try</u> to learn English before you disrespect and/or talk to me, please. It would make it a lot easier. No, you can't have deal. Why should you get a deal? Just because you come from another country doesn't mean you should get a deal. Or is there another reason you feel you should get a deal? You don't like my tone? Then burn it and get the fuck out. The people who agree with this will eventually out number you people who don't, if the people who agree don't out number you already. So take the ashes of this and stick it as far up your ass as you can reach.

I am through going for the knees. From now on I am going for the throat. You can shoot and stab me as many times as you want. Even though my body may die, I will live on through my work. Because death is just a myth to me. So, I will go for your throat and nobody will hear you cry out because my work will drown your cries out.

An American walks in to where I work and yells like Dennis

Hopper in *Apocalypse Now*, "I'M AN AMERICAN!" We all scatter but he catches one of my co- workers and yells, "I WENT TO YER...YER SUPER DRUGS...AND I HAD TO WAIT IN A LINE FOR FIVE MINUTES BECAUSE SOME OLD LADY WAS MOVIN' TOO SLOW! I WENT UP TO HER AND SAID "LADY, YER AN IDIOT!" AND I LEFT AND CAME HERE. DO YEW GUYS HAVE ONE HOUR DEVELOPING?"

My co-worker says, "Yes, what is your last name?"

He yells, "AL!" and leaves. His clothes were a few decibels louder than his words in the heat of the summer.

That was the last American I dealt with, and you all wonder why everyone hates you.

I know what you look like. You are cramped down, ugly and small. Dying by your own ego's now frail hands. I don't need to help you die anymore. I set the wheels in motion and now you finish the job that I started by being the one who returned the favor of treating me like shit, by treating you like shit. I know what you look like.

It is impossible for me to make this shit up.
Seriously, it is impossible for me to make this shit up.

I forgot murderers.

First murder conviction gets 20 years in prison and counselling. Second murder conviction by a male gets his legs, arms and penis amputated. If it's a woman, she gets her legs, arms and breasts amputated. Simple as that. Simple as that.

I don't want to get evicted, but I demand and deserve respect from you.

If you don't like it here then shut your mouth and go back where you came from.

Oh no! You just hit the paradox!

I have gotten a permit and I have enough money saved, so soon you will have to watch your ass.

Epoch.

I have come to the realization that I can't afford to move. So no more bitching. I will stay in these weeds (only physically) and when you least expect it, the ripples from my work will hit you in the knees and the throat and knock you over.

Epoch.

I am only recognized by people who don't recognize me.

Epoch.

Call my work "art" and talk down to me again and I will cut both of your thumbs off.

Epoch.

I noticed that you couldn't even sign your name you chicken shit. I won't give you any pleasure by responding to your blowhard shit. Epoch.

When you wake up in the morning from last night's adrenaline rush from last night's drive by shooting, don't even bother why we think all orientals and middle easterners are terrorists and/or gang members. You give a bad name to all of the decent orientals and middle easterners. Don't even bother apologizing because it's far too late for your drivel. Fuck you. I'll see you in prison.

Epoch.

Fuck you if you don't agree with some or all of this.

Epoch.

Mark the day you start reading this on your calendar. Because I am coming to hunt you down like the stray rabies filled dog you are, when you finish this.

Epoch.

Fuck you.

Epoch.

<u>EPOCH!</u>

-JUST DESSERTS-

Epoch.

It has been said before by many people who are far more intelligent than me, but I will say it again, disrespect is a two way street. What goes around, comes around. Karma or whatever you choose to call it is fine by me. So don't be surprised when you spit in my face on a daily basis that I come after you with an aluminum bat. Will you regret your actions then? Welcome to Babylon fucker. You want to wear that attitude on your biceps out in public, then what's the difference between you and the Nazis with swastikas on their biceps?

Disrespect is a two way street. What goes around, comes around. Karma and you will get exactly what you deserve. Remember this before you die because I will be the one etching it on your tombstone:

"THEY GOT WHAT THEY DESERVED IN THE END."

Remember this fucker. You will get yours.

Epoch.

-AND PAY FOR YOUR CRIMES-

This was written ages ago.
This was chipped into stone by elders.
This was carved into wood by medicine men.
This was written on parchment long before your saviour was even conceived.
This is spray painted graffiti done on walls under cover of darkness.
This is saved archivally on all of your discs, cds and hard drives.
And when you turn it up, open it up, decipher it and read it, you will regret every second of your miserable life.
And when you are at your lowest point I will come to tell you that you are of no use to anyone anymore and that you must live another thousand years for your crimes. I will tell you the secrets of despair.
FOR I AM THE KING OF MY HATRED AND YOUR DESPAIR
This was written ages ago and uncovered seconds ago. I give you my respect for reading all of this, this far. You can't turn back because if you do I will attack you from behind, and if you face me, this is what you get. Spit in your face.
I will release this once I have become a hardcore recluse and you can't find me. Even if you do, you wouldn't recognize me and you would be powerless to stop this. I am dead. Officially.
How do you justify this? You can't. Try justifying a child screaming because it can't ride the purple and green alligator in the shopping mall. Try justifying homophobic assholes. Try justifying teenagers raping a mentally challenged girl with a broom handle and a baseball bat. Try justifying rural racist rednecks who discriminate just because of the colour of skin and/or tattoos and/or hair styles and/or other minor differences in people. Try justifying child molesters, murderers, rapists, etc,. etc,. etc..
Well...what do you know...I just justified this by accident. Well... what do you know?

Epoch?

The End.

Epoch.

The End?

started "for windows" piece on
may 12th, 1999.
finished this piece on
june 23rd, 1999
in edmonton, ab
refined on christmas
because christmas is the time for giving
and sharpening knives.

-*"For Windows" afterword*-

    Ah...where do I start? First I have to say that re-reading this piece after all of these years, I find myself agreeing with most of what I have written. On the other hand, some of what I have written makes me ask myself, "What the fuck were you thinking, Corey?!" Some of the writing that I do not agree with is as follows: "...a typical bitch woman." (page 6) or "...all the lesbians i meet are bitter and/or screwed in the head...." (page 9). The previous statements are blatantly wrong, which I see now.

    That being said, at the time I wrote this piece I fully believed everything I wrote. I was working in a dead end retail job in a camera store in a very busy mall. The management were tired of me, as much as I was tired of them and the customers and some of the staff. I know that there is no excuse for sexism or homophobia, but at the time I had experienced several incidents which polarised my views on my life, other people's lives and society. Secondly, why did I put this at the end of the piece instead of the beginning of the piece? Had I made this "afterword" a "foreword" I would be letting the cat out of the bag and at the same time (maybe) making you the reader's view of this piece negatively polarised and maybe even take a pass on the rest of the book. Not that I would have minded that, but I would like to think that the rest of this book does NOT seem so sexist, homophobic, xenophobic, etc. At least that's what I would like you to believe. Thank you for coming this far. I hope that you enjoy the rest of the ride. Thanks!

#1040

You can't tell I am raining
If the sky is crying

#853

DRAGONFLIES

In a dream
I was driving down a dusty road
When I dreamt of dragonflies
That were bigger than my arm
And they fluttered gently
Around my feet
Around my "careful not to step
On their beauty" feet
They were blue and green
The dragonflies were
A blue/green that you only see
In a lake at the foot
Of a mountain
On a clear sparkling sunny day
In a dream
I was driving down a dusty road
Watching my large yet delicate
Friends
Flutter around me
Almost as if they knew
That I could fly with them
In a dream
Or in reality

#828

VULNERABLE

I hope that you had
A good day
I hope that
Even if it was cloudy
Outside
It was sunny inside
I hope that
If you thought of me
It did not bring you down
Because I am
Feeling very vulnerable
So if you thought of me
I hope that it
Brought a gentle smile
To your gentle lips
And I genuinely hope
That you had a good day

#813

MY AFFECTION

I don't want you
To hang on my every word
They can't support you
You might as well
Go for the emotion of
It all
Because words
Are just tools of mine
And emotion is the
Building material
For my home
You have to find
It all
Inside yourself
I can be
And sometimes maybe
Of some help to you
But for
It all
Look inside yourself
And you will find
It all
It all

#911
WHITE LAUNDRY

Her eyes are like a whisper
And they watch over me
Where ever I lay
I sometimes wonder
If she thinks of me
This has so many pages
So much so that
How could one forget
It must be time
To roll up my sleeves
And go to sleep
For that is the only way
For me to pass the time
Until her return
Though I know full well
She will never return to me
So she will remain
As much of a memory to me
As I can only hope
That I remain to her

#238
FROM UPSTAIRS

She said to me
"She could marry my man
And it wouldn't scorn me
For he is just a
Burning cage to me"

And she was a cynic
In a field to me
No love, no hate
Just a stare which said
"You're just a friend, not a mate"

But you don't understand that
Sleeping is like dying
Except when you sleep
You waste time you deserve
And dying they take back
All of the time that you've earned

#1146

THE OUTSIDER

I read a book today
It made me feel like
I had just woke up
From a multi year coma
It made me mad
At all the people
Who call me a friend
Then never call me
Or ignore me in public
I don't have friends
I have a holocaust
Full of acquaintances
Who insist on fucking with me
When I open up to them
So I draw more inward
And never trust anyone
Except myself
My first
(And only)
Girlfriend
Dumped me in the shower
And never told me why
She didn't love me anymore
So to this day
I would still like to ask her
What went wrong
And why she used her venom
On me
When I tried my best
To be her friend
Oh well what can you do
I read a book today
It made me angry
At how you lied to me
Just to bait me into
Telling you the truth
After I tell you the truth
You become one of my
Holocaust friends

Living where I stay
I have lost all hope for humanity
I see no light at the end
Of this tunnel
And my past has caught up with me
And culminated in
My current attitude
(Bad or otherwise)
Living where I stay
I am constantly asked
For my money
By pissheads
Who don't give out income tax receipts
I am constantly harassed
By ignorant disrespectful
Smoking drunks
I am constantly ignored
By anyone I try to be friendly with
And constantly pestered
By people who think
That they are being friendly with me
But are actually being nosy
And should be buried alive
Under that new old folks home
That they are putting up

I read a book today
That made me want
To re-read all works on alienation
So that I know that
Someone else feels like me
At one time
Even if it was for a brief moment
I am not happy to broke
All of the time
But I got used to it
I am not happy to have been molested
But I get by O.K.
I am not happy with my holocaust friends
So I will have to meet better people
Or get used to it
People flip out the words

"Never get used to it"
But eventually we all
"Get used to it"

I read a book today
That made me feel some hope
In myself
Hope
That I would be at peace with myself
And that the people I meet
Would stop the games
And just be at peace with themselves
So that when they meet someone
Who has dug in deep
They don't feel threatened
When they see their own weaknesses
In the mirror
After the chance meeting with myself

#960

QUITE DESERVING

I don't deserve your art eh?
Once you put it out
And make it public
Then everyone deserves your art
So make up your mind
There is no such thing as
A last symbol of deceit
Because everyone performs
Some sort of deceit
At sometime
Don't make idle conversation with me
I get that everyday
And it bores me
The page is blank
And you can't make amends
Because I have been reading
Too much Machiavelli
Or maybe
Not enough
When concerning you
And your art

#1167

HOLOCAUST FRIENDS

I have said this before
I will say it again
Until you shut your fucking mouth
Once and for all
You...
Wait a minute
I'll call you
You...uh...don't have my number
You call me, I have to go
But you never gave me
Your number
You are a Holocaust Friend

Hey, you know
If you ever want to try
Me as a boyfriend
Oh...
We're just friends
You have never once called me
Even though I have given you
My number several times
And you have never given me
Your number
You are a Holocaust Friend

I consider you
A friend
A casual friend
So don't read into it
Anymore
Alright
I knew I should have
Not even tried
To bother with you
We are not casual friends
I am an acquaintance to you
You are a Holocaust Friend to me
And I have one thing
That I kept from you

Your number

Holocaust Friends
I have got all of your numbers
And it is only a matter of time
Before I brand you with them
And throw you out into the street
After you have finished your sentence
Then all I have to see
Is your number
And I will know that I already
Have your number
And I can pass you by
Without apologizing or flinching
Because in my eyes
You are dead
Or at the very least dying
Holocaust Friends

#1157

E & B IN A & E

A woman asked me for change
I said NO
A man in front of me
Gave her some
On my way home
I saw her buying cigarettes
See what your altruism got you?
It made you happy you helped out
The under-priveleged
But you just fed her addiction
I have seen many out stretched hands
And unless they give out
Income tax receipts
(And that's pushing it)
I have turned them all down
The virtue of selfishness
Unless your well being
Directly affects my well being
Then fuck off
Break altruism

I have put myself on display
Several times
In reputable places
(For their time)
And I have been bombarded
By snobs
Who think that if your meaning
Isn't deep
And you aren't abiding by
Their bullshit elitism
Then you have no right
To call yourself an "artist"
I have entered your elitist world
And I don't like it one bit
I am an artist
I just won't play by
Your pretentious rules
I would rather keep my

Friends and interests
Than bury my head in the sand with you

There is a fine line
Between altruism and elitism
And I try my best
To walk the middle
You have too look out for some people
But not everyone
You have to look out for yourself
But not to the point
Of the exclusion of some more visceral
Interests you may have
And do not look down on anyone
Just because they work on instinct
I have entered altruism
I have entered elitism
I have tried to break altruism
I have tried to break elitism
And I have not entirely succeeded
You may have won the battle
But eventually
I will win the war

#830

EPITOME

I should have seen this
From miles away
Now I wonder
If I am just a souvenir
It's not a joke
This is how it is
If you think
For a split second
That this poem
Maybe about you
Then it is
And if you have
Any doubt
As to our relationship
Then you know
That this is
Directed at you
Do not
I repeat
Do <u>not</u>
Come to my funeral
You are not welcome
In my life
And most certainly
Not welcome
In my death
This is not a joke
I am not a novelty
I am not souvenir
I am not a prize
I just <u>am</u>
And now I know
You are not
I should have seen this
From miles away
You should have seen this
From miles away

#931

AT YOUR DISCRETION

You are a cannibal
Of the moment
So I am leaving it
As I found it
Take over
It is your's
Do I make you nervous
By my stare?
Do I make you anxious
By being as honest
As I can be?
Don't take uncertain future
For granted
For it will never
Be the same
After you let me in
Socialism and
Communism and
Fascism
Have the same ending
Mediocrity
You are a cannibal
When it's convenient
I am a cannibal
Because I have to be

AND MYSELF

I get my feelings
From a dispenser
At the back of
A run down empty warehouse
I was thinking
We could go outside
And try to find
My laughter
Because giving up
Never felt so good

I have my feelings
From a dispenser
At the back of
A run down empty warehouse
So if you're looking for me
You have to look
Long and hard
It used to be easier
But that was way back when
I used to promote myself

I got my feelings
From a dispenser
At the back of
A run down empty warehouse
Where unfinished marble sculptures
Keep my path from deviating
From the honest truth
That the whole day
Is almost as lonely
As the whole evening

I gave my change
To a dispenser
At the back of
A run down empty warehouse
And after completing this task
I walked slowly out

Realizing that
The dispenser in the empty warehouse
Continues to make me
Keep distance between you

And myself

#864

HOWARD ROARK

Take whatever road
Will challenge you more
And don't give me
That line that
They are all equal
Because if I have
Only learned two things
In being alive
One is that nothing is equal
And the second
Is that if you take
The weaker challenge
Then you will become
A weaker person
Instead of a stronger one

#240

SNATCHED

I don't know how to react
I'm not happy but not sad
The knot is still strong

Around my forehead's reach
Around my forehead's reach

Spies and flowers won't know
How I am nor am I
But neither will I

Know who I am nor am I
Know who I am or am I

I knew him a little
(Little is not much really)
I wonder if he felt the same

I'm not sure anymore
I am not sure anymore

Thinking over and over
Staring up and down and all over
I wonder if he really cared

.#615

JUPITER

For some reason
I just can't cheer
When another planet
Is being beaten to death
Long after he's been forgotten
In 1994
I will remember
Carlos Delgado's season
Things happen
And they're not
In anyone's control
So we make
Them a milquetoast or a martyr
We usually only remember the bad
And never the good
What was that young kid's name again?

#1048
THE THOUGHT POLICE

"I will not have you thinking that way about our clients 13802," spoke Jack 43204 sternly to Dade 13802, "I know that warren 85271 can be hard to deal with but thinking he is an 'asshole' that close to him could cost the company a great deal of revenue. So when Warren complains, action needs to be taken."

Dade 13802 guarded his thoughts closely (so as not to get in any more trouble) and in a somber tone replied, "Yes sir, I'm sorry and I won't let it happen again."

"I hope so because I value your production for the company, you are a valuable employee but I won't tolerate such disrespect from my staff. How about this, I can feel you are upset so why don't you take the rest of the day off? We will manage...you just go home and try to relax, maybe talk to your T.O. about your pacifiers and such and come back tomorrow with a clean slate. Alright?"

"Yes sir."

"Okay, see you tomorrow 13802."

As Dade 13802 was showing himself the door, Jack 43204 spoke in a grim tone one more time, "Next time, keep those thoughts in the warehouse in the back, not the front office. Please and thank you."

Dade went through the back instead of the front as he usually did. Going through the front he would be able to see Laura 62834 but that is how he got in trouble in the first place. Being in the front on lunch instead of the back. Passing all of the "drones" (as Dade liked to call them) with their dulled happy thoughts and their dulled happy smiles and their dulled conversation, one of them brightly (and unknowing of what transpired) smiled and slowly waved to him. Dade didn't respond as he left the plant.

It always bothered Dade when Jack called everyone, except the buyers (customers, clients, assholes, whatever) by their numbers instead of their names and how he tried the benevolent ruler thing but could never quite pull it off. He was a ruler alright but benevolent was the opposite word of what Dade was thinking.

"What can you do? A lot of things bother me lately," Dade mumbled to himself as he went to catch the bus.

There's the 14:39 bus, I'll be able to get home 2 hours earlier than usual and I won't have to see that woman who snapped at me one afternoon a few days ago...or was it a few weeks ago...in the morning, doesn't matter. I loved her hair (I hadn't been off my off my pacifiers long) and right after I thought that she burst out in an angry tone, "You just want to grab my breasts!" and stormed passed him to the back of the bus. I was so embarrassed because everyone was starring. Maybe she wasn't on her pacifiers either and that's why she jumped to conclusions. Everyone jumps to conclusions (except Laura) when you try to be nice. Maybe they see something in me I am missing and I sure feel alienated and alone. Whenever stuff like this happens I get so full of such self doubt because no one trusts anyone anymore and when you're open like me maybe people don't know how to respond. Here's all the doubt again, maybe I should be taking my pacifiers but I don't want to be a drone anymore. I really believe that I'm better off without the drugs.

Adjusting his respirator and sun blockers Dade mumbles aloud, "how long have I been off my pacifiers? 1, 2, 3 weeks...or more," people start staring and he just sticks his tongue out and continues to himself quieter now, "the old memory is not so good because of the pacifiers, or lack there of," giggle giggle quieter yet," that's the problem with not taking the "happy bastard drugs" as I like to call them." Now the whole bus thinks I need a nurse, more uncontrollable giggling.

The scientists who made them, O.K., happy drugs, pacifiers (no happy bastard drugs sound better, Dade thinks which draws a smile to his face) whatever, can figure out how to keep everyone in cruise control but can't figure out why the mind reading all started and how to stop it completely. Which is it I wonder? Being on the bastards screw your memory up, or not being on the drugs screw your memory up. My memory is good enough to keep me on an assembly line but not good enough to help me remember how many years it's been since the ozone crashed, pollution, chemicals in the water, food, land and air and whatever else has caused all of this crap. I mean we can't even get fresh (let alone organic) food anymore. It's always bio this and bio that. Has anyone ever thought that maybe all of the stuff in the food and water has caused the mind reading?

My mind is racing so fast that I forgot that his "boss" told me to see my T.O.. Thought Officer! What can my Thought Officer do?! Give me more pacifiers or send me to prison or better yet therapy! If I could afford to move into a house, or even a condo, I wouldn't have the T.O. coming every Friday. I heard that if you live in a house they only come once a month at the most! That would be awesome! No live-in T.O. and more privacy. What a change for the better! Stop dreaming...with my paycheck I will never be able to afford a house or even a condo.

There's that oddball who gets to ride for free. He always reeks of stale beer and urine and his clothes look circa 1998 or even earlier. Must be nice, I have to pay and he freaks the drivers out so they let him get on without paying, must be nice. How does he get away with that crap?

"Because I can shit head, now mind your own fucking business," he says in an ominous voice only Dade can hear.

Dade adjusts his face protection, rings the bell and gets off at the next stop. It isn't his but he has had enough.

I've got to be more careful, Dade thinks to himself, he read me like a cheap novel. My mind is just racing now, the walk will do me good and then I will have a nap. Even as the bus pulls away he can still feel the bums intensity.

"That's the only good thing about the pacifiers, they help to disguise your thoughts," he mumbles.

Good thing I am getting off early because I won't have to see that girl, or is it a woman, I can't remember, anyways she always looks depressed. Finally I get up the courage to ask a perfect stranger if she is O.K. and she just ignores me. I could feel that she was thinking I wanted something else besides to try and help her. I just ended up turning around and watching her back shuffle off. Ever since then she walks on the other side of the street when she sees me coming.

"Take some more happy pills people," Dade says aloud as he takes the first few steps up to his walk up, "people always jump to conclusions nowadays or maybe I am just to sensitive," he says in a barely audible whisper.

Ah...home with all the dirt and break ins and cockroaches. Oh the cockroaches are huge as well as some other insects like silver fish and such. At the beginning of the end of the ozone someone said that the bugs would out live us and they are probably right. Unlock this door and got to the couch and rest.

Just what I almost suspected when I left the plant, a note under my door.

Dade walks in and reads the not and slams the door when he is finished. It says:

"I will come and see you after you get off work and get settled around 18:30. Talk to you soon. -Steve 72803"

This is getting better by the minute, I wish he didn't know my schedule so well. Jack 43204 must have snitched on me because I can't see Laura 62834 doing that, she's always been so pleasant to me. I mean

I just went up to chat with her to break up the monotony (I don't know which would be more monotonous, assembly line or answering phones all day) and asshole walks in. I was just trying to make her happy in some way maybe we could get together because I am so lonely all of the time and she's always smiling at me and now I know I made her uncomfortable because she looked down when I thought that word about Warren 85271. Laura wouldn't snitch, but if she read my mind then probably Warren did and probably he told Jack and now here I am.

The worst part of it all is that Laura probably doesn't want to talk to me anymore. My mind is going so fast I should just lay down on the couch. I know it's barely 15:00 but I need to rest. I am getting so confused, so angry, so sad, so tired...

Dade 13802 lays down on his couch and drifts into a restless sleep as the cockroaches come out of hiding while the coast is now clear.

The knocking at the door woke Dade 13802 from one of those deep sleeps that leave you all sweaty and confused about what time it is and where you are the few moments after you get up. Dade answers the door and it's Steve 72803 the resident Thought Officer.

"Hello Dade 13802, did I catch you at an inconvenient time?" The question sounded as if he didn't care if it was inconvenient or not.

"No..uh..yeah...no not really, I was just napping and I forgot that you wanted to see me, that's all." Dade stumbled his way through his response still disoriented from his "nap" but he tried to guard his thoughts as best he could.

"Well I won't take up much of your time 13802," the T.O. spoke cautiously, "We are concerned about you and your best interests. You don't seem to be yourself lately and the flash point of sorts was earlier at your job." 72803 was now talking in a low monotone voice which didn't help to keep Dade awake one bit.

"The reason I have been thinking about you and now speaking to you is to see if you are or are not taking your pacifiers. Are you or are you not taking your pacifiers?"

"No", mumbled Dade a little defiantly.

"I see, why is that?"

"I don't know, I mean I don't want to take drugs anymore, I want to be clean."

"And you think that they wouldn't have helped you in the situation earlier at work today?" Steve 72803 asked condescendingly.

"I don't know, maybe. I mean it was just a slip of the mind and it could have happened to anyone," Dade13802 said defensively.

"And what about your low opinion of your job? You seem to complain about your job, your products you make, your people you work with, your pay and the list goes on and on. Some of this is internally spoken and some times it's externally spoken."

The Thought Officer seemed like he was trying to provoke something or show Dade 13802 something or maybe Dade was just being sensitive again.

"Of course I complain, I feel guilty about doing what I do, wouldn't you? We make land mines, not teddy bears!" Dade 13802 was beginning to get defiant, "but jobs are so hard to come by and I was in a daze on the pacifiers so I took what I could get not knowing what I was getting into."

"You were not guilty on the pacifiers, were you? Are you sure you won't start taking them again? I am authorized to give out a whole three months worth to you."

"Yes, I told you I want to stay clean," Dade 13802 was getting edgy and it was coming through in his voice.

"You are being quite difficult and we may have to send you for therapy if you don't start taking them again."

"Fuck you! I don't like being threatened, asshole!" Dade spoke vehemently. "People are always coming down on me for my views and actions. Even if they don't involve them. I don't see why I can't keep to myself and everyone else keep to themselves as well. I am trying to fit in, but you and the likes of you are always putting thoughts into my head that I don't agree with. I don't do it to you, why do you do it to me?" Dade 13802 paused in anger and then started up again, "Don't answer, you have the authority and I don't. It seems like everyone else has authority to do and say as they please but me. So if you want to send me to the pest house I..."

"Medicenter," interrupted the thought officer.

"Whatever! The likes of you seem to have these clean names for things that don't seem so clean to me. I mean I have never met anyone after they have gone to the "Medicenter" for some "therapy". I find this extremely odd. There must be someone out there but in my work or down time I have never met anyone. What goes on in those places? What are "we" hiding?"

Silence. Endless silence. Or so it seemed to Dade 13802 until there was a knock at the door to Dade's apartment. Dade 13802 couldn't figure out who could it be because he wasn't expecting anyone this evening. As he was pondering this the Thought Officer spoke up, "I will get the door, it is for me."

Dade 13802 felt a sense of dread when T.O. Steve came back with three large men dressed in white, "Nurses," whispered 13802.

"We expected as much and decided that you need a short break with a little therapy. 13802."

One Nurse went on 13802's left side, one on the right and the one Nurse stood in front with a large needle in his hand, he nodded and the nurses on either side gripped 13802 so tight that it hurt. The nurse slowly pushed the needle into 13802's right arm, which was being held the tightest, and injected the serum.

13802 said sarcastically, "So much for staying clean," as he slowly drifted away his last words to the Thought Officer were, "Yeah I feel guilty about my job, do you feel guilty about yours?"

72803 just smiled as 13802 drifted back into a deep sleep. As the five of them left the cockroaches and silver fish and the likes were now able to roam freely.

At the nearest Medicenter, 13802 is wheeled into the office of a therapist on a gurney.

"The last one for the day", boomed Therapist 58064, "We have met our daily quota of dissidents. You may now leave the room while I sever the nerve fibers of his frontal lobes. You have all done well." The therapist proceeded with the last therapy session of the day as well as the first and last therapy session for 13802.

A nurse and therapist walk into a fairly quiet large room with four rows of chairs with six chairs in each row. The chairs are all filled with people of all ages and genders. They all look like they are heavily sedated. Slow moving, if at all, mumbling to themselves and a few are gazing skyward and drooling. There is a large photograph of a flower on the wall in front of the wall that they are all facing.

The therapist asks one of the men, "20016, how is the flower today?"

20016 responds in a low monotone voice, "Very pretty, thank you for asking."

The therapist asks one of the women, "68079, how is the flower today?"

68079 responds in a low monotone voice, "Very pretty, thank you for asking."

The therapist asks another one of the men, "13802, how is the flower today?"

13802 responds in a low monotone voice, "Very pretty, thank you for asking."

THE END

started this piece on
august 24th, 2000
finished this piece on
august 27th 2000
refined on new years day
in edmonton, ab.
because that's when you make
resolutions.

#1043

It is just after 5:30
In the morning
And there is a thunderstorm
Rolling outside my window
I love thunder storms
Early in the morning
I could stand in the rain
And proclaim to the sky
I love you

#1003
HOPE IS A LOTTERY TICKET

My interview with hope
Keeps on getting postponed
Right when I show up
So I end up having to go home
With my tail between my legs
Getting out of my best clothes
And relying on a lottery ticket
That I can't afford
The bells tolled twenty eight times
One for each year I have been
Alive
I just wrote this down
At night
Until I dropped into sleep
I listened for someone
For hours
To put an end
To this perpetual prayer
No one called on me
The night seeped in the windows
And the hope went out
The back door
The night is long
The hope is shorter
And I fell asleep knowing
That the interview is futile
When hope cancels itself
And I go missing every night
I come home
It doesn't hurt so bad
This has been happening
Every time I go missing
The morning comes early for me
And I get into my best clothes
Hoping that hoping comes into style
And I won't have to
Give up on something else again

SNIPER

#780

The persons and events
Portrayed in this production
Are fictitious
No similarity
To actual persons
Living or dead
Is intended
Or should be inferred
The persons and the passions
Portrayed in this production
Are fictitious
The events and lovers
Portrayed in this production
Are fictitious
Families, friends and bystanders
Portrayed in this production
Are fictitious
So now I see my face
Buried in a cardboard box
On the side of the road
Near a sex scene car crash
Are fictitious
I have such a cacophony
In my home
I can't breath or
Talk to my lovers
Are fictitious
I am so cool
And popular in this little world
That I enjoy waking up
Every morning rain or shine
Are fictitious
The ending to this
Will be so happy
I will never write another piece
Are fictitious
I am so content with my life
I will never write again
Are fictitious

I will never write again
Are fictitious
Are fictitious

#767

DO YOU WORRY THAT I DON'T LIKE YOU DO YOU EVEN CARE I KNOW ABOUT THE WEATHER SO I DON'T KNOW HOW TO START BUT SOMETIMES I KNOW HOW TO FINISH WHAT SAY WE START AGAIN LIKE WE NEVER MET AND SEE WHAT HAPPENS WHEN WE TALK FIRST AND ACT LATER INSTEAD OF THE OTHER WAY AROUND BECAUSE I DON'T KNOW ABOUT THE POWER OF LOVE I KNOW I KNOW I KNOW I KNOW I KNOW NO KNOW NO KNOW NO WHERE I CAN HOPE THAT A WARM LIGHT WILL BE ON WHEN I GET HOME I KNOW NO KNOW ALREADY THAT THE TRACK MARKS ON MY ARMS ARE INVISIBLE SO WHAT DO YOU KNOW NOTHING WHERE TO LOOK WHEN TO LOOK WHY TO LOOK I HATE I AM SITTING IN A CAFE WISHING THAT THAT BEAUTIFUL YOUNG WOMAN AND HER FRIEND WOULD COME SIT WITH ME IN MY HARSH HEAVY LONELINESS EXCEPT MYSELF ACCEPT MYSELF HAVE SOME DREAMS AND YOU DON'T WANT TO HEAR ABOUT THEM SOUND LIKE A BROKEN RECORD OR A SKIPPING CD PRETEND NOT TO CATCH MY EYE YOUR EYE RAMBLING RAMBLING DYING DYING SLEEPING RAMBLING DYING NO CURING NO CALLING NO CALLING NO CALLING.

#621

I AM

I write this
After the first time
I meet you
I met you
I met you
In a dark cafe
That I've only been to
Once or twice in my life
I sit in a corner
Think to myself
Thinking to myself
I hear a familiar melody
Go through my head
And wonder when
The last time I heard it was
And that's when you walk in
And that's when I
Thank my lucky stars
That I am not making this up
It all starts with a smile
And ends with a conversation
I wish I could write about you
The way real poets do
It's more flattering that way
I wish I could write about you
The way Goethe or Cohen
Would if they met you
For the first time
If they felt the same way
I feel about you
I wish I could write about you
The way real poets
Of past or present do
It's much more flattering
Than anything I can do
Or that's how I feel any ways
I feel like
You have the same effect on me
As does a song by Kronos Quartet

A passing mood that
Breezes right by and through you
Leaving you feeling
Refreshed and with a clean head
I really wish
I could talk about your eyes
Or your golden hair
The way real poets do
But I am still a half poet
Who every once in awhile
Has his peace pleasantly disturbed
By someone like you or
By my writings
What else can I say but
I hope that I will meet you again
And we can talk further
Freely again
Not having to worry about
Offending each other
Because it's just talk
Because it's just opinions
And neither are meant to hurt
Neither of us
I wrote this
After the first time
I met you
I met you

#1154

INFATUATION WITH INSPIRATION

Art
Any art
Inspires me

Music
Neil Young Bob Dylan
Ani Difranco Black Flag
Black Sabbath Nomeansno
Mississippi Fred McDowell
Kronos Quartet Crass
And much much more
Inspires me
Music inspires me

Movies
Meryl Streep Robert DeNiro
Beatrice Dalle
Hitchcock Orson Welles
Coppola Kubrick
Martin Scorsese
And much much more
Inspires me
Movies inspire me

Writing
Ayn Rand Kafka
Goethe Bukowski
Aristotle Joyce
Paglia Machiavelli
And much much more
Inspire me
Writing inspires me

Painting
Duchamp Juan Gris
Warhol Colville
Hockney Barbara Kruger
And much much more
Inspire me

Painting inspires me

Photography
Mapplethorpe Mary Ellen Mark
Man Ray Ansel Adams
Helmut Newton Ken Jarecke
And much much more
Inspire me
Photography inspires me

Music and movies
I am not that good at
But at least I have tried
But the other three
Are just the opposite
The names above inspire me
For different reasons
But they inspire me none the less

But the name I left out
Who inspires me the most
Is
Corey Wayne Hamilton
Because if you can't inspire yourself
The most
Above
Everyone else
Then why wake up in the morning

Me
Any me
Inspires me

END TO END ACTION

#701

I learn more
From people's silence
Than their words
Words are just make up
To disguise one's muscles
Twitchings and runnings
Uncomfortable silence
Silence forthcoming
Uncomfortable silence forthcoming
To thwart your pitiful attempt
At hiding
Your true thoughts
An uncomfortable silence
Is your response
When I speak my mind
And don't mind my speak
This is how I am
Don't mind me
This is how I am
Don't mind me anymore
Because I know
That there is a fine line
Between dead silence
And white noise from
One's mouth
Both show ill at ease
I try to walk a line
And say
Only what I have to
Only what I feel
I have to
And leave the rest
Locked up for myself
So have some silence
And I will learn from it
All you have to say

MAYBE NEXT TIME

#1148

You would swear it's fall in Vancouver
When you tell me that that's where
You are from
And you tell me
That your skin is now happy
And I would like to touch your happy skin
And see if its happiness
Would transfer to me
Even a little would help a lot
Because I am so frail at night
And this is when we talk
I would like to get to know you
But I am so shy
And lately my past
Has caused me to burn up
On re-entry
I would like to move to Vancouver
But someone who stole
Part of my childhood
Lives out there
And I am scared
That I would get worse out there
So I stay here in limbo
With everything moving so fast
Except for me
I would like to get to know you
But I am afraid
That if I do
You will move away
And I will have to start over again
I would like to move to Vancouver
But I am afraid I would just get more bitter
About her and just more angry
About her and just get more sad
About them
And what they put me through
All of this has caused
Me to be shy
All of this has caused

Me to feel alienated
Where ever I go
I hope that they die slowly and painfully
And I hope you forgive me
For saying this and
For being so shy
Maybe next time
We can talk more
Maybe next time
When you get off from work
I waited awhile
While you were at work
I knew your shift ended soon
And I know that this is obsessive
You were talking with a man
Who dressed much better than me
I waited awhile
I think you noticed me watching
So I walked away
Letting you talk to the handsome man
In his handsome clothes
And I just caught my bus to work
Feeling sad and lonely
Now there is snow and ice on the ground
And I feel myself slipping away
Just like the recent unseasonably warm weather
Where does this shit come from
Maybe next time
I could ask you
But you would still be talking to the
Handsome man in the handsome clothes
And I am too shy
To interrupt and ask

#747
AUTUMN'S FALL

The hair
That you touched
Has been cut off
The skin
That you touched
Has been washed
Clean
I can no longer
Smell you here
Amongst myself
And my desires
I desire you
When I am
Near you
Far away
I crave you
Like caffeine
Or alcohol
I could smell you
But I know
That you said
It first
What to do
On this night alone
What does it matter
What you say about people
For they make their
Own minds up
About history
Whether ancient or not
This is now history
And I am alone
Re-reading it
And I have made up
My own mind

#1042

PORTRAIT NUMBER ONE

You will hide from me
I should throw this away
And let it be
But I just can't rest today

I have got more
And you have got to know
About my score
And just how much I will hoe

I am a gardener
Tending to my garden
My garden is a painting
And it is a painting of you

I just cannot rhyme
When I write about you
So I will bide my time
Until this is through

I got stuck in a rut
When the first one left me
No if and or but
It just happened to be

I am a gardener
Tending to my garden
My garden is a poem
And it is a poem about you

I do not mean to sound
Like Leonard Cohen
But I cannot make a sound
And you will not let me come in

All this makes me want a drink
Not drinking and driving
Not time to think
Just drinking and hiding

I am a gardener
Tending to my garden
My garden is a photograph
And it is a photograph of you

I am a gardener
Tending to my garden
It is a garden all season long
And it has been quite some time
I have been this gardener
Tending to this garden
And the only one to see this garden
Is the gardener

#681

SALTER

I am trying to work late
To make me forget that
I like everything centered
And in the centre
There once was a person
In the centre
But now that person
Is missing
With hay stuck
In the under carriage
Of the car
And blood all over
The outside and inside
Of the car
And inside a briefcase
Is a photo tag
I once handled
And <u>she</u> once handled
Before <u>she</u> went missing
Before I went missing
On my way back to work
One day
On <u>her</u> way back
On <u>her</u> way
To work late
I have to work late
I have to work later

#650

MY TOES

Sitting
Now in the warmth
someone else's home
In Saskatoon
I think about
The four rolls of film
I took
And how it ended
The day and the film
I crossed the street
To see three children
Moving railroad ties around
Near a basketball net
In an abandoned
Parking lot
I start taking some pictures
When they notice me
Two of the three
Come running up to me
They are young aboriginals
One boy and one girl
And they are very young
The girl is so cute
And has a smile that
Melts a part of me
That I hold dearly to myself
They ask me what am I doing
I tell them
The other boy
(Aboriginal too)
Jogs over
The first two tell me
That they don't like it
And that I scared them
I felt very bad and
I explained that I was there
Shooting a bit for the
The Saskatoon Blades hockey team and
The Saskatoon Star Phoenix newspaper

This makes the three of them
A little more happy
I then let them take some pictures
Show them how to
Load and unload film from my camera
And take the camera apart, etc.
I tell them that I am a student
And so on and so forth
They tell me that they thought
I was a cop
And that cops had come
Into their home
Late at night
And they didn't know why
I ask if they are in school
The oldest boy is in grade 6
His sister (the one with the smile) is in grade 5
And the other boy is their cousin who's in grade 4
The cousin asks me
Why I was taking pictures of them
I said that because they are interesting
The cousin asks me
To take pictures
Of those people over there
I reply that I don't want to
The cousin asks why
And I say that they aren't interesting to me
And that I think that
All of us white people look the same
(I guess I was just trying to be witty)
And I ask if they agree
The other two stare at me blankly
The cousin responds
"We're all human"
I felt like an idiot
And look down at my toes
The girl asks
If I would like to come
And take pictures of them
On their teeter totter
I say yes
The girl and her cousin run off

The oldest boy watches
Me gather my stuff
He asks if I am rich
To own all of this equipment
I tell him no
I just got a loan
By this time
We have walked over
To their teeter totter
That the three of them
Have made out of railroad ties
They ask me when
I pay the loan off
I say soon
We chat about hockey
And football
I ask if they have been
To a Blades game
They say in unison "No"
The cousin says
That he had seen
The Edmonton Eskimos play football
(He has just moved from Edmonton)
I reply that I have never seen
The Edmonton Eskimos play football
But that I have seen
The Edmonton Oilers play hockey several times
The three of them gasp
Simultaneously in awe
I take some more pictures of them
The cousin asked me
So many questions
That I lost track of them
And I wasn't able
To think up answers fast enough
The next question is easy
It's the same as before
Take pictures of those people over there
The girl quickly responds
"You ask too much"
And she smiles that melting smile at me
I can't remember their names now

Only their words
Their faces
Their bodies
And their actions
They say that it was nice to meet me
As they run off to play pool
I shout the same after them
And I can't remember their names now
Only their words
Their faces
Their bodies
And their actions
Their bodies
I hope that nothing else bad
Happens to their tiny
Aboriginal bodies
I am scared for them
So I try to think
Of how they made me laugh
Of how the cousin
Was disappointed that my car
Was an Acadian
And not a Stealth
I try to think of the happy things
And smile as I think of
Their bodies
Their actions
And their words
And the oldest boy who didn't talk that much
And his younger sister with the smile
(That I pray I captured on film)
And the younger cousin who asked too much
And said "We're all human"
I will always remember
Their young innocent intelligence
That made me smile
And look at my toes
At the same time

#989

The hope
Can't stand the silence at night
The labels do
The labels
Can't stand the noise of day
The hope does

#1047

7:30pm, Saturday August 19th, 2000

Listening to music now. Watched a biography on Bob Dylan. Really interesting. I learned a lot I didn't know. I would really like to see his music collection. Sold some photos of Old Reliable to Mark of the band. I gave him the photos, he gave me an Old Reliable t-shirt, a R.L. Burnside cd and $8. I'm happy with this. Mark said he had heard the Catie Curtis quote too. She said, "I want to go back to Lillith Fair," about being surrounded by men at her Sunday work shop. What an asshole thing to say...I hope that it was a misquote, but if it wasn't and she doesn't want to be surrounded by men, then she had better not leave her home. I felt like a dork after I read that comment on Monday because I met up with her at the Folk Fest and told her how much I liked her stuff. I knew I shouldn't approach other artists I don't know but like because they'll just treat you like shit. Not all of them, but most of the artists I have met from Ani Difranco in 1992 to present seem like they've got huge egos or if that's not the case they have personal problems and take it out on me. I know it must be tough to be in the public eye and have issues, but don't take them out on me, the paying fan. I hate people who have problems that don't involve me, but take them out on me. That's so unfair. If you have a problem and I'm causing it, tell me and I'll do my best to stop it, otherwise leave your shit at home in your toilet.

PEOPLE JUST UPSET ME.

#1085

Hum along
To your drinking and cocaine habit
And I will dance along
With your beautiful naked body

#1112

She makes me
Never want to buy or rent
Or even look at
Pornography ever again

#1090
ALREADY SPENT

About this time
Yesterday morning
I was walking outside
To catch a bus
And I see a fat old dirty man
Go riding by on a bike
Built for a twelve year old
It was low to the ground
And had a banana seat
He was carrying
four or five bags with cans
And such in them
There was snow
All over the trees and lawns and cars
But the streets and sidewalks
Were just wet like it had rained
He sped by
And dropped a plastic
Car oil bottle
As I was walking
Closer to him
He circled around
To pick up the plastic container
He did so
And continued to circle
Until we were close enough
To talk
He asked me if
I could spare a few cents
I said no
And continued to walk
He just rode off
Into the cloudy spring morning
With snow on just
On the trees and lawns and cars
And I just walked on
To catch my bus

#1138
HISTORICALLY CORRECT LONG WEEKEND

On a long weekend
It started out dry
And in the middle was wet
I drove with my family
Where no planes land
(Except the ones you walk on)
And stayed with my roots
They fed me
And let me stay
The whole weekend
I met people
Who recognized me
Who had never met me before
There were no reported contracts
And they let me eat
With my hat on
The sky was the bluest blue
And the cattle stood
On the greenest grass
Near the clearest marsh
No one judged me
For my tattoos and hair style
And I was able to bitch about pro sports
And the weather and other things
And I made friends easier
Than I have ever before
The pace was slow and easy
They probably talked behind my back
But I know what it's like
They are all like older siblings
Who are worried about you
I didn't have to worry about
The traffic, the fakes, the junkies, the drunks
And all of the others
Who don't like the clean air out there
This was the middle
And it put me at peace
The twelve hour drive was dreadfully honest
Starting out dry

The middle wet
And going to the end of this trip
Was dry again
So dry it caused forest fires
But we trudged along
And when I got home
I ached for next year
But next year I would
Listen even more
See even more
Shake more earnest hands
Give and receive more of
The most genuine of genuine hugs
And sleep easier than I ever have before
For there are no
Traffic fakes junkies drunks
To point out that I have a hearing problem
This was the best long weekend
I have had in unrecent memory

#1142

JUNIOR HIGH SCHOOL

I noticed the other day
That when I was running home
Running to escape from my job
There was a tinkling sound
Coming from inside my chest
I guess that's what happens
When you are constantly given a hard time
At work

There was a tinkling sound
Like a bunch of stuff was broken
Inside my chest
I know that what happens next
After the running and the tinkling
Is the scarring
The scarring is the worst because
It lasts longer on the inside than on the outside

The day after the tinkling and scarring
I spent all of my change I could scrounge up
On a heart that doesn't feel
It was on sale for 95 cents including G.S.T.
Regular price was the life of another
But this one was reduced to clear
Because they aren't that hard
To come by

So the heart transplant went well
The 95 cent heart was considerably smaller
And I had to stay invisible
For a shorter than usual time period
But it worked out well
The day after all of this
I was back at work
Ready to take on another day

Just in case of any trouble
I brought a lady bug to work
It was the size of a small tomato

I figured that if lady bugs eat aphids
(That's why they're my favorite insect
For they are so beneficial to the environment)
That it would eat all of the people
Giving me grief at work

It didn't work
I just ended up hurting the lady bugs' wings
In transport
It was still alive but it just couldn't fly
I cried over this and went home early
For the crying thing wasn't supposed to happen again
With the 95 cent heart
So on the way home I took it back

It was a stretch
To get my old heart back in
But it worked out O.K.
This just goes to show you
That one shouldn't look for deals
With the heart
Hmmm
Maybe I should cancel
That brain transplant appointment

#1101

I saw a crow
Perched on a tombstone
Today
While I was on the bus
I thought to myself
That there must be
Some significance to this sight
But any meaning behind it
Was just out of my mind's reach

#1099

RAY OF LIGHT

I went to do my part
For the environment
And recycle my recyclables
And I ended up waking up
Some young teenagers
Sleeping in one of the dumpsters
I wish I could offer them more
Than reprieve from the
Sun and the wind
By closing the lid
But I can't
And I went home
With the sight
Of a young dirty girl
Blocking the light from her eyes
With her tiny dirty hand
I will always remember this
Because I felt so guilty
For buying a slurpee afterwards
When I could save the money
To better myself
By helping them out
By opening a home
For the homeless
I would probably
Still feel guilty though

#1106

The sky
The clear blue sky
Could offer me a home
And I would graciously accept
For there is no greater gift
Than a home in a clear blue sky
No matter if it is warm or cold
It is still the greatest gift
A home
A peaceful home
In a clear blue sky

#1110

IN THE SKY

On my way to work this morning
While on the bus
I saw two rainbows in the sky
One was much brighter than the other
So I watched them until they both faded away
The sky was a dark brooding back drop to them
So the brighter rainbow lasted much longer
In the sky than the other
I felt as if I was the only one
Watching them
As if
They were meant for me and
No one else
They were meant for me
To let me know that everything
Will be O.K.
That everything will work out
Just fine

#1115

I liked you so much
That when you lied about
What I did
I did it
To make it a truth

DREAM FLOWER #2

Listening to Johny Cash
I remembered a dream I had
About a flower
I don't remember the smell
But I remember the texture
And the colors of the lush petals
Purples, violets and magentas
So I painted a painting
That only I see the flower in it
But that's O.K.
Because it makes me remember
The dream and all of the
Other flower-likes
I have dreamt of
I have smelled and touched
And been blessed by their beauty

#1135

THE HUNGRY NINE

Listening to this music
Makes me think about you
Makes me think about
How much I love you
And how much you love me
And this barrier that's
Between us
But that's O.K.
Because you smoke and drink too much
And you want to travel
Or live on a sail boat
Just off of your island
I want to move closer to you
But not too close
Because of my fear of loving you too much
And either not getting it all back
Or getting loved just the same
But I know it will all be fine
Listening to this music

Listening to this music
Makes me think about my dad's mom's brother
Who played baseball with eight others
Called "The Hungry Nine"
They played ball in Manitoba and Saskatchewan
Entertaining the families on sunny days
He ended up coming down
With the same disease I have
He ended up dying with it
But hopefully he was at peace
With himself
Knowing that he made
A lot of people happy
This is what I think of
Listening to this music

Listening to this music
Makes me nostalgic
And the facts get blurry

But that's O.K.
Because isn't that what's
Supposed to happen
When I am
Listening to this music
Isn't that what's
Supposed to happen
When we all
Listen to music

#718
A CHANCE STONE

I am walking on
Sharp stone of silence
It is a hard working change
When the hostage
Takes the hostage taker
Hostage
But I can't take it away
Because I don't know
What love is
For I always wonder
If you ever let
My kind
Inside of you
If I approach you
It is with trepidation
For my courage
Needs a roof
And my heart
Needs a brace
I am not a hostage
Or the taker
I am a giver
I can only give you
An open mind
For you to make
A difference in
And hope that
You accept it
In good faith
And can return the favor
In kind
Then the stones of silence
May become
The sands
In my dreams

#739
CAJOLING A RESPONSE

If your actions
Mean nothing
Then why do you
Do those actions
It is a fact
And a warning
That another man
Is coming
For my heart
And your body
Watch in the rain
And you will see
His foot steps
On the pavement
Don't come in
I won't let you in
Both of you
Cannot come in
My door is locked
And I am safe
From both of you
I pick up the phone
I didn't hear a ring
And there you were
On the other end
Walking away
I tried to hide my cards
But I was
Never any good at cards
So I let them
Fall on the floor
And unlock the door
And let the place
Go to shambles
I have no one
And I can't go out
Unless I have
A camera
It makes everyone nervous

And stay away
If your actions
Mean nothing
Then mine
Are heavier
But just like the man
Who comes
To persuade me
To go his way
No one sees me
And I just
Crumble away
Like dust
From a thousand
Yesterdays

#920
OPPOSITE APOCRYPHAL

It is my oppression
It is in my guts
I started to enjoy the pain
Because it is the only
Pure constant in my life
I realized this
When I saw a dreamer
Screaming in a store window
So I bit my bottom lip so hard
It bled in my mouth
So I bit my lip
In anticipation
Of all the waiting I must do
Till I make something
Of myself
It is a personal affront
When you put my stone
Next to your breast
And I taste the salt
In my mouth
While a shadow
Looks up on my back
And the owner
Of the shadow
Tries to be my nightmare
Fait accompli
Serving the liquid damage
On the solid damage
Help me
HELP ME
I've lost my diary
The one I have never used
In it
Is my oppression
In it
Is my pain
It is constant screaming
By a dreamer
Crouching in a store front

With shattered glass
All about him or her
Of which I am not sure
It no longer matters
Because I spit the blood
Out of my mouth
And wipe my lips
And strike out
At the owner of the shadow
Knocking the owner
Into all of the damage
Liquid and solid
And walking away
With my head up
Fait accompli
I no longer need my diary
And I am no longer worried
About my stone
For I am walking away
With my head up
Fait accompli
Fait accompli

#811
LIVING MEMORY

Yesterday
You went shopping
On my spine
And now I will
Shoot tomorrow
Because my life
Used to be in stereo
But history
Left me behind
And when that happens
You stumble around
Aimlessly
In a sort of daze
It could signify a lot
Meeting a woman
Named Autumn
And then leaving
Much too early
I didn't want
To make anyone
Uncomfortable
Especially her
But ever since
I found out
Joy died
My politeness
Has crumbled like
Autumn's leaves
Under foot
I only knew him briefly
But he never did me wrong
So what can I do
I am behind an eightball
When I meet
Someone as
Beautiful as Autumn
Because I never know
How to be myself
Without offending

Someone
This is so scattered
And abstract
That it barely
Makes sense to me
Joy died a month ago
I left Autumn
Much too early
Joy is dead
And now
Winter is upon me
When It is
Well into spring

#766

The paper flutters
To the floor with exclusive rights
To no one
But the man
Hammering on my door
Telling me to turn down
That god-damned noise
Little does he know
That this is the most quiet
It has been in here for years

#912

VOX POPULI

I have been living
Without it for years

Struggling

This is not a pat
On my own back
Am I so different
That the wind
Always seems
To blow at my front

Struggling

With no control
And not a lot
Of room to live
Because they take me
Nowhere
That I want to go

Struggling

In these fifteen minutes
Before a game
Of loneliness in my bed sheets
Thinking that I am
A special gift wrapped up
For anyone

Struggling
I am made to be shameful
By others
And the worst
Myself
I make myself lie
To others
and the worst
Myself

Struggling

To find myself in this mess
I feel so close
To it and myself
That I am called an egoist
I chuckle to myself and
Clutch my cards
Tighter to my chest

Struggling

And finally

Yielding

To myself
And my own
Personal desires
That struggle within
To reach out
For myself

Yielding

Only when it suits me
Making sure
That I am sure
That this is sure
And all that is
Is sure

Struggling

Is sure

Yielding

And I am sure
It is sure
That I am young

And the struggle will go on

Yielding

When I am through

Struggling

When I am through

Yielding

To others

Struggling

Against others
Only when I am through

Struggling
Against myself

Yielding

Against myself
To be one
With myself
I have been living
Without it
For years

Yielding

HAPPY BIRTHDAY YOUNG ONE

Don't follow me
I won't follow you
Hear no evil
And you'll hear only one side
I am patient
I will sit and wait
And watch for you
Unknowing what will happen next
In the bar
In an "alternative bar"
Alone on a friday night
Watching people dance alone
And together
Kissing alone and together
When it occurs to me
That this scenario
Has (and is) happened (happening)
To someone else
Somewhere else
And they are writing it all down
Almost as furiously as I am
And I wonder if they are thinking
Of what Kafka would do
If he were in the same position
And then it occurs to me
That maybe it did happen to him
In his own time
In his own way
He wrote it down
In his own way too
On top of this
And all of my scribbling
I wonder if you'll come alone
Or with one of many people
But I guess that's why
These places are so popular
Because everyone
Looks so beautiful
In the erratic lighting

Real today
Unreal tomorrow
Or vice versa
Which ever I am not sure
Are you bored?
No I am alright
Are you bored?
I am alright
Do you want to go?
NO I AM ALRIGHT
Do you want to go?
Yes
Okay, fine, I'm gone
Are you going?
Yes I'm going
Are you going?
Yes I am going
Are you going?
I AM FUCKING GONE ALREADY!!!
I was feeling
A third wheel anyways
I say it all
I say it all
I know the scene for tomorrow
When we no longer look beautiful
And the music isn't
Pounding in our ears
I am going to get it in the ears
With all the degrees of a police interrogation
And there is no way that
I am going to kick this out
I'm guilty of something
But I'm not sure of what
When I answer the phone
After I've driven away
In a mad fury
And slept so light
That my own breath woke me up
After all of that
I won't be as sharp
But I will be honest
But I think I've figured out

What I'm guilty of
Staying around too long
Being noticed way after
When I am not supposed to be noticed
You will only hear one side
And a little of mine
Than all of a sudden
The quality of the phone service goes down
Hello
Hello
This connection must be bad
I'll hang up
And continue this
When your foot
Is over my line again
Goodbye
Goodbye
As usual I am over reacting
As usual I am over looking something
And it's at this time
That I see a vision
Of your mother cradling me in her arms
Telling me what I should have done
Telling me what I should not have done
As usual my visions
Are too little
Too late

#728
INNOCENT BYSTANDER

I am tired
Of starting with myself
This all started
With her leaving
With all of the stress in December
On her shoulders
And leaving
Before any words
Of comfort or advice
Could spill from my tongue
Gently into her ears
And then there's
The young girl
Working at the flower shop
Who makes me wish
I was a young boy
So I could experience
What I missed
In my youth
She doesn't believe me
When I say I have
A crush on her
And then there's
The other young girl
Saying yes to seeing me
Next day comes
She brushes me off
Like you would
Brush the dust
Off of your pants
After you have taken
A nasty spill
And wish to forget about it
I am tired
Of starting with myself
And wish to forget about it

#829
AGENTS PROTECTED

I sit in the back
Because I am shy
I mostly keep quiet
Because I am mostly meek
I let my writing
Be the outgoing one
Because you don't know
A damn thing about me
And that's the way
I would like it kept
Most times
Most times
I just let it all go
Falling backwards
Into my lonely bed
And let my nightmares
Break me down
I end up waking up
Hoping
Waiting
To see your shadow
On the floor
But all I got was
A letter yesterday
Asking me
What luxuries
I could afford
And all I could afford
Was an explanation
As to why
I am always alone

#973

BELIEVE ME

Next time
When I come
I hope that you believe me
When I say
That I have come
To see you
For I would never lie to you
I have nothing to gain
By lying to you
But possibly much more to gain
By telling you the truth

#413
LOVE AND MAGIC

Smooth ripples
In green calm water
Smooth pores
In pale cool flesh
Slow movements
Like fish
Sliding through
The calm atmosphere
Thoughts
Thoughts are passive
And human
And soft
Melting
Slowly
Into one
Calm rhythm
Calm actions
Calm one
Calm all
Touch the silk
Touch the cool breeze
Of a rare
Peaceful moment

#223
THE ANSWER

The answer is
What you think it is
So little hot ashes
So big red tape
But it's loud and it
Crashes
Through your head

The answer is
What you see it as
It's that burning heat
It's that freezing cold
But it whispers in your
Sleep
And on your ears

The answer is
A huge conflict
And conflict is dramatic
And you must figure it out
While it smashes through
Your attic
But you'll get it soon

For it's so obvious
The answer is
That there is none
No certain answer
Until you're done

BUSY SIGNALS

I had a love song
But I left it out
By accident
And it went all mouldy
I walk down
The centre of the street
When bugs start
Falling on my head
And I thought that
It was like
I was partnered
With an undesirable
In my sleep last night
But it had
No relation to you
And I saw a man
With long black hair
Who looked sad
Then I noticed that
A small patch of hair
On the left side and
A larger patch of hair
On the right side
Were shaved almost to the skin
There was no balance whatsoever
And it was never revised
I hate you for not saying
That my honesty will cost me
Maybe if you had came out and said it
I might have some respect for you
I lost my memory
And that's why I can't sleep
I lost my memories
And that's why I can't wake up

#558

THE ENGINEER

The area outside
Is getting
Smaller and smaller
She mouthed the words
"I want to go"
And I thought
Where?
But I kept my
Mouth all tight
And squirmed
In my seat
And felt
Like I should hide
And I tried on
An uncomfortable smile
And I passed
She passed
Right on over me
I'm so young
I feel like
I know Oswald
Personally
And his wife
Is even closer
To me
Than he was
I knew her face
Or a face like it
In those
Black and white
Photographs
Support the struggle
I'll support mine
Not yours
Thank you
You're not
Worth the trouble
Cut him and
His wife down

I'll cut you down
If I thought
You were worth it

Opening a mind
That's been
Closed for years
Is virtually
Impossible
Trying to correct
24 or 25 years
Worth of mistakes
Is virtually
Impossible
Chew on that
Swallow it hard
Oswald
His wife
I never knew
Them at all
And neither did you
You needed a frame
And I needed the picture
You stole it all
From me
You stole it all
From his wife
Worst of all
The area outside
Is getting
Smaller and smaller
Get your own damn chair
I've got mine
Now you get your own
Like trying
To teach someone
To colour inside of the lines
When I've never
Been able to
Pull that one off myself
I kept my mouth
Shut so tight

And until now
I was polite
But my manners
And my smile
Passed right on
Over me
Over you
And out the window

And when my grip
Tightened on my seat
While you tried
To pull it out
From under me
It was seen
As bad manners
Oswald's face
Was muted
By his wet cheeks
I can't forget
Both
And I can't
Defend both
I am being crushed
By my own anger
And your embarrassment

#584

LEGALIZED MEAN

I am crawling around
Looking at underexposed negatives
With just one drop of water
On and in the centre of my left shoulder blade
Won't someone help me
Won't someone help me
I am trying to write stories for children
But I don't know anything
About stories or children
Another drop of water lands on my left bicep
I am naked and warm
But I shudder anyways
Thinking about what I just burned
And the story I am trying to write
I always thought that stories
Were supposed to be fictional
Aren't stories supposed to be fictional?
Keep writing
Keep writing
I like you thinking that there are two of us here
But I point out that there is only one of us here
Breath deeply
Breath deeply
I am not just trying to be this way
I used to have a good grip
But now I have just slipped again
I am smelling like a stranger again
I don't know or understand what is going on
But I do know that I want to help someone
But I don't know if anybody wants my help
Or if just nobody knows that I want to help someone
I wonder to myself
Why wolves always sound so sad
And I want to meet
Richard Roe and John Doe
Richard Roe and John Doe
Are you okay?
Do you want people to ask
Are you okay?

I am crawling around
With droplets of water
On my naked body
Wanting to help someone
Anyone
Wondering who nobodies are
And why certain things
Always sound sad
And after I dry myself off
And get dressed
And try to move on
Ignoring the questions
That are throbbing to be answered
I write down to myself
That an idea in the
Middle of the night
Is the same as a dream
In the early morning
You won't remember either
Unless you write them down

#288

BOYS

Well it's the end of
Another shitty day at work
It's only Wednesday too
I've noticed that I have
So many problems lately
Some big some small
But they all seem to
Grind on and at me
You know, I wish
I was five years old
When you're that young
Everything around you is either
Too big or too small
You are so small and so are
Most problems
Most problems
Just slide right off
Then when you get older
Reality kicks in and
Kicks on and around
Oh well, I guess that's
What happens when
You send a man
To do a boy's job

#919

INTERDECEPTION

You can't have my pallet
You are not worthy
Of such a gift
Because I was dreaming
Of your man
Calling me and speaking
In a language that
I didn't understand
So I called him back
And I told him that
I was going to shoot him
In the only language
I knew
It was mine
And it always was
And it always is
And it always will be
And I told him that
I was going to shoot him
In the face
And leave him to rot
For you
That will be
My gift to you
You are worthy
Of this gift

IT'S YOUR ACCENT

#601

Silence doesn't
Bring on questions
Questions
Bring on silence
I don't need you anymore
Because men of low opinion
Of the world
Usually have high opinions
Of each other
You waste my time
When I walk the streets
And read your quotes
On the front page
Of all that trash
You just don't get that
Private life is not
Public property
In your game of takers
Play seriously
Will you
Play seriously
Because if you don't respect me
While you're alive
Then why should I respect you
When you're dead
It's harmful
To imagine you
I can hardly wait
Until I get home
And away from
A memory of you
That's the last time
I thank a hero or heroine
Maybe it's not organized to you
But it is to me
You don't understand it?
Then put it down or
Read it again
And I was just thinking

The other day that
I wasn't going to call you again
And then I run into you
Somewhere
I don't want to run into you
Too much time around you
Is harmful
To my imagination
To my image of you
I can hardly wait
Until I get home
And away from a memory of you
It's like
I was partnered
With an undesirable
Again
In my sleep last night
When I walk down
The centre of the street
And bugs start
Falling on my head
Again
Yes
I eat meat
Does it matter
Does it matter
That everyone is mashing together
Does it matter
You make me hate
You make me hate
This city
You make me hate
My life
You make me hate
Myself
This is true
You make me hate
Yes,
You make me hate
I don't want your eyes
I don't need your eyes
Because I am a blacksmith

I can see perfectly clear
What I am forging
You can't

#952
LET IT GO

A dirty old man
Is digging a grave for me
In his dark damp cellar
I will greet him
At the porch of his house
And he will bury me alive
This is my ace
Up my sleeve
For at least I know
He cared enough about me
To dig a grave for me
And bury me alive

#546
WHERE'S YOUR NAME

She told me
She hated this book
As cliche as it sounds
I feel like
She hates a part of me
You sound just fine
Why do deaf people
Have names
I wasn't sure
What to call it
Until you gave it a name
There sure is a lot of
People looking out of windows
Watching me fall down
I fall down a lot
Do you have a name
Because the
Transaction has been made
If it all wasn't real
It is now
The deal is done
Signed, sealed and
Shellacked
Don't hate me
Shellacking
It wasn't a
Liquid document
I gave to you
It was solid
Very solid

#640
MY OWN FLANDERS FIELD

I never saw the man
After the end of last week
He went M.I.A.
And I had some work to do
I have these scars
And they're just killing me
So I think I'll put on some war paint
And go start a war
Just to fit in
Well the fighting's
Been fierce
For thirty days or more
And I finally found my first victim
Face down in a sewer
I rolled him over
And discovered
That it was mister M.I.A.
I didn't feel sad
I didn't feel angry
I didn't have a care in the world
My war was still on
And I was no worse for wear
Times are getting tough
And I don't know what to do
I can't get through a sentence
Without forgetting a word or two
You laugh at me now
But you are my next victim
My shadow is leading me on
And before you know it
You'll be face down too
Now I know
I am just a reflection
Of what has happened to me
And that society
Is just a reflection
Of my actions
Well it started as a personal war
And I can't tell you what will happen

In the future
But I hope it hasn't been done
Because I hate being bored
And I don't need another gun
And when I re-read this
I can't see it going any place
But six feet under
And I wrote on the bottom of this page
"Where is this going?"
And I wrote on the bottom of this page
My true response
"I don't know"
And I almost wrote on the bottom of this page
My last thought about this
"This poem is virtually pointless"

#1144

PARIAH

You didn't have to ask
But you did
And I wished that you were
On a closed circuit television
But you did
On a national broadcast
And I nearly saw their tears
I nearly saw tears
That nearly came
But I only saw nearly tears
You have interviewed
One two many million dollar snobs
In your time
And you forgot
That their nearly tears were
Under nineteen and they
Were all amateurs at this
I felt their nearly tears
At letting their country down
These girls were
These girls are
Women heroes to me
To put up with your ignorance
And I hope
Although I even know that
In your time
You will get yours
For their time is now
And their future
Burns all the paths
To your past, present and future
You didn't have to ask
But you did
And that is why
When your road
And their road
Cross again
They will stand tall
Just like I saw their skyscraper height

When last you met them
Except this time
Your questions
With any luck
Will bounce like my last rent cheque
And they will see you
For the fool you are
And they will know
That the outcome of the past
Matters nothing
To the brightness that their future holds
You didn't have to ask
But you did
God speed young ladies
God speed

PARANOID?

#586

I was told
First tell them
What you're going to tell them
Then tell them
What you want to tell them
And finally
Tell them what you told them
When I hear things such as this
I feel like sitting
Cross legged on my kitchen floor
Thinking all sorts of jumbled thoughts
Name of a magazine
He hasn't got a tooth in his head
"The End" was carved
Into the back of my chair
And all of a sudden
There is a little bit more heat
And one jumbled up piece
Falls in my lap
Telling me that
I should notice it
A little more than the rest
That you were
In the opposite lane
With a median between us
It used to have
Grass growing on it
But now they put
Black asphalt over top of the grass
And I used to want to
Be in the same lane as you
And I wanted your hand
On my head or on my arm
But now it's just an
Old, worn out photograph
Fraying at the edges
With no negatives left
Just an old photograph
With frayed edges and stains

I was asked
If I knew about the three domains
Affective
Cognitive
And psychomotor
I didn't really
I always felt that
These domains made someone
Say things like
Previous achievements
Are our present stains
Anything you do now
Will affect you later
These are all predispositions
That want me to wear white
I wear black instead
To absorb light
Not reflect it
I know already that
Life is a compromise and
That inhibitions are restrictions
I know all of that
These domains are all very repetitive
They say of that over and over again
It's like those are the only things
They can say with any amount of confidence
Can't you find any new material
Or do you have to keep on dragging
Up all of those anachronisms
I mean
Maybe it's right in your time frame
But it's way off of my time line
I keep on thinking you'll
Find something new
To impress upon me
But I know that sort of hope
Is like crossing the road
And starring into the eyes
Of the drivers in their parked cars
Seeing if any of them will recognize you
And honk their horn at you and wave

It never happens
When you want it most
And even when you need it most
It most times won't happen
These sorts of congregations
Seem to think
That they know exactly
What I will do next
Like they calculated
It all out last week

And now they'll sit back
And nod in content
As I perform in the way that they expected
If this is the case
Then how come after
I do my own part
All I see is the black holes
Of mouths open wide
And all I smell is pure unrestrained shock
I am not patting myself on the back
I will leave that up
To the people who think
That what they typed
Into their adding machines is correct and true
And I sometimes wonder that if
Those tiny chips of metal
And circuits of plastic told them
That compost is a fruit dish
If they'd believe in it
Or go see if it's true for themselves
I am not patting myself on the back
When I say and do
Everything I say and do
But I started it all in a modest way
And it will take eons
For me to refine it and complete it to my liking
I am not even sure myself how it will end
So how could anyone else

#1145

Do what I say
Because
You have nothing
Better to do

#1094

Oops!
I've forgotten what causes
I would die for
I just hate it when that happens

#1156

Oh
I'm sorry
Did I just kill you
It was an accident
I can assure you
It will not happen again

#1123
FOOTPRINTS

If you didn't want a heavy weight
Dropped on your foot
Then you shouldn't have stepped over that line
It makes me think about how much
I like walking in the winter
When it has just snowed
And I walk in it
And when I cross the dirty roads
I leave perfect white footprints
On the unperfect dirty roads
It looks so absolute
But I know that this small accomplishment
Gets washed away with the traffic
So I just thank my lucky stars
That I can do this on a perfect winter's day
And it makes my day perfect
And how much this accomplishment means to me
Because this helps wash away
What I have had to do to you
Because you went over that line
And I had to show you that
My boundaries were momentarily overtaken
I know I go to extremes
But I know that soon you will wash it away
Just like my perfect footprints
And we can move on
And that is the beauty of friendship
And that is the beauty of our friendship
We can move on

#1140

BEING CATHOLIC

I cannot follow
Your design
I cannot buy into
Your beliefs
I cannot comprehend
Your insecurity
I cannot understand
Why you would be so discouraging
To one's own responsibilities to one's own actions
The things
You put me through
Just because of my pride
Just because of my work
The things
You put me through
Are disrespectful
And to use a direct quote
"Disrespect is a two way street"
The things
You put me through
Give me stomach cramps
And an earache
My purpose
Is my work
And my work
Is my purpose
You are so tired of me
You are so tired
Yet I am wide awake
Even though
I haven't slept in years
I still remember
The last time I slept
Was the last time
People like me
Made sense to
People like you
And even when we did
No one was listening

Because you gave up from the start
So my kitchen is infested
With tiny insects
And no matter how much I clean
They won't go away
So you couldn't see me turned around
Using your mistakes
To disinfect and kill germs
No one is listening
To the crowd that is at bay
No matter how much
They yell
In a sort of a mechanical drone
I was just interrupted
By my phone ringing
I saw on my call display
That it was you
I never answered
Because earlier in the week
You left a message
On my answering machine
Asking if my old Nirvana ticket stub
Was for sale
You wanted it so you could say
That you were there
With us
The first and only time
That they played here in this tiny town
I let you leave another message
And keep on counting
On what I keep
That is special to me
So I can't complain
When I let my guard down
And drift off to sleep
Letting my dreams
Of bitchy co-workers
Irritate me in my sleep
I could be that way too
But I just can't fake it
I am not brilliant
I am of average intelligence

I am not gorgeous
I am of average looks
By the way
It is not my mistake
For being average
The higher you raise the bar
The farther it is to fall
With that piece of gorgeous intelligence
It is a wonder you get out of bed in the morning
I think to myself that
The more people I meet
The more I like myself
You think that's funny
You think that's fucking hilarious
I'll show you what's fucking hilarious
A photograph of this dead derelict
I took years ago
Oh yeah
He had your morals shoved up his ass
Because you preferred
To talk about you
Thinking all day
Instead of
Thinking about you
And then talking all day
Your sympathy is so strange
It's not like you
Your sympathy is usually reserved
For those who you consider needy
Look where it got that derelict
Abstinence is like utopia or anarchy
One man's view of either
Is different from the other's
Heavy petting can't compare
To the real thing
So you would prefer
Some teenage girl getting pregnant
Or a S.T.D.
Instead of using a condom
You fucking idiot
You obviously had the sex drive
Of an earthworm

When you were that age
Or you never had any peer pressure
It really takes me down
When you throw the so called good book at me
Awkwardly I hide out
It passes time until
I draw the winning hand
And say
I don't need your brand name
To get by
Look at him
Look at him
He is just like that derelict
I mentioned earlier
Look at him
Look at him
Do you think he knows
What it's like to be a teenager now
Do you think he even remembers
What it was like to be a teenager then
I would say
Don't make me laugh
But I started laughing when I was a teenager
And I am not laughing
With you
I am laughing
At you

#642
WHITE OUT FORMULA

And I hope that
My words
Will ring in your ears
For years to come
So when something happens
That I warned you would
You will hear my voice
Trying to comfort you
It will be trying very hard
For it will have the urge to say
"I told you so"
And I hope my words
Will help you
Like you helped me
I have to move on
And I don't feel
That you are able
To move on with me
I have to start my own movement
And I have to start it so quick
That I have just jumped
Out of my chair
Knocking it over
As I rush out of the room
To begin my great things
For I have just realized
That I am great
With or without you
These are not daggers of spite
They are the truth
A truth that you always found
Hard to swallow
Why this was
I am not sure
There are several maybes
That come to mind
But the one that rings the loudest is
Maybe you couldn't swallow
Because your throat was too tight

Too tight because of
Your lack of direction
And you saw that
I had a direction
And you have none
With all that said
And done
I hope that my voice
Could give you
Some sort of comfort or help
Because I myself
Cannot

#1092

CHALLENGE

I am getting good
At writing down
As few words as possible
But at the same time
Saying as much as possible

Now
What are you going to do about it?

#1150

PLAGUE

Sometimes
I don't care
If you think I am talented or not
Or if I am happy or not
Or if the candle is burning at both ends
Sometimes
I don't mind if
I don't have as many books as you
Or if I don't talk amongst ourselves
I don't feel obligated
To follow your rules
Go save yourself
I'll walk where I want
I'll sit where I want
It is an operation
That I will conclude
When I want
I am in total control
Was there ever any doubt
If there was
It was a figment
Of your imagination
What goes around
Comes around
You will get yours
I was never in the middle
Because it's always too tight
To turn where and when you need to
I am not asleep
I never was
And never will sleep
I don't need to
Because it is not worth it
I can't afford to lose the time
In not producing
A positive let loose
And my work
Keeps me wide awake
I will be back

It is inevitable
Maybe not here
But somewhere else
You can put your life savings on it
And after it's all done
You will double your investment
And never need to work again
Yes it's worth it
You will know it when it comes
Because I know how to work it
Like 3 mile island
Slowly taking everything over
Until you have to start all over
In the next century
Maybe even longer
Because my focus is so sharp
It has laser precision
And it will cut through you
Like a hot knife through butter
Drop the sometimes
I just don't care
I will say it once
And that will be the end of you

#933

OSTRACISM

My name is exile
I am in exile
From my own body
My body is exile
From my own mind
My mind is exile

One day
A young lady
I work with
From nowhere asked me
"As a guy
What's it like
To be on a constant
Hormone high?"
My response was as follows
"I am mildly offended
By your question
So I will ask you
As a woman
What's it like
To be bitchy
All of the time?"

She apologized
But I can't accept
Her apology
Men who say such
Are not men
They are boys
Women who say such
Are not women
They are girls
They are all children
Except young children
Sometimes can't be held
Accountable
Adults always should be
Accountable

I shouldn't be angry
But somebody is
I shouldn't be bitter
But somebody is
I shouldn't hold a grudge
But somebody is
That somebody is
Me
That somebody is
Me
Her actions
Were unprovoked
By anybody
By somebody
That anybody and somebody is
Me

My name is exile
I am in exile
From my own body
My body is exile
I am in exile
From my own mind
My mind is exile

I am in exile

#357
DEBTS AND OBLIGATIONS

More lies
As you torture us
With an axe
Over our heads
Tear and torn
Abused used all up
Till we are dry
Then you say
We owe you
We owe you
Fuck you
We owe you nothing
You owe us
Respect
Respect for all we
Have done for you
Respect
You owe us

TSUNAMI

I am not sure how to start this
It begins by me thinking
About me feeling
That I never had a mother
And this gives
Me an excuse
To be so intense
Walking on someone's face
Is not proper social behavior
Know your enemies and
Watch your friends closely
There's so much
Unwarranted trust floating around
Open your own fucking door
And case the joint yourself
I am through fucking around
With your nonsense
"Have you seen the lord?"
"Why, yes, I did
Just this morning in fact
While I was shaving
I saw him in the mirror
And that's:
Have you seen the lord sir, to you."
And then all that walks away
But you know I love you babe
You know I love you babe
But you can't trust your memories
Because memories fade
It all comes second
In an extended cab
With an all points bulletin
Telling me that Kurt Cobain is dead
I am not sure how to finish this either

#956

SYNCHRONICITY

This has been rewritten several times
So you understand it clearly
That cold night in March when we met
I was stood up by my maker
I never told you this
Because you would have
Just let on like you cared
When you never did
So I let you take me to your home
I paid you your money
And we had sex
And you got angry at me
For not getting off
So while you were getting dressed
I shot you in the back of your head
Smiled and patted your child on the head
And gave your roommate a ten dollar bill
For her troubles
Then I left
Drove home
And went to bed
With a smile on my face
Just another busy week night for me

This has been rewritten several times
So you understand it clearly
All day at work
I put up with you
Persecuting me for having a dick
After I let you into my car
After I drove you to your home
After you got out of my car
I shot you in the back of your head
I dragged you into your house
Politely greeting all of your roommates
I put you into your bath tub
And talked to your dead body for an hour
Left
And went home and listened

To shitty dance music for an hour
All the while in the background
The telephone was ringing
I ignored the phone
And went to bed
With a smile on my face
Just another busy week night for me

This has been rewritten several times
So you understand it clearly
You are a registered nurse
No
You are a hair dresser
Who wouldn't give me the time of day
Who would give me a glass of water
If I was drowning
Well I was drowning
And I got out of that trouble on my own
I hunted you down
I found you
I seduced you
And after you went to sleep
I rudely woke you up
Rolled you over
And I shot you in the back of your head
I dumped you at the salon you work at
Walked in
Got my head shaved
And left leaving a hefty tip
Just another busy week night for me

There are cemeteries full of these people
There are bodies filling the streets
I walk through them all
With a smile on my face
And a skip in my step
Because I always get the last laugh
I used to be a drag
Guess what
I still am a drag
I just keep to myself more than ever
Care for you was gently deposited in a garbage can

On my way home
My voice carries
Yours never will
Because if my back is turned
Then your purchase is lost
And when you dice me
For the first time
It will be the last time too
Because I bought a gun
And now my weeknights are busy
And I always go to sleep
With a smile on my face

#1020
SET THE RECORD STRAIGHT

He said
"It is not titles that honor men
But men honor the titles"
Think about it
Think about it
I don't have to tell you
Twice
It hasn't changed
I wait for you to leave
Because it will be
One of those days
I will forget quite easily
Step up and admit it
And maybe I won't
Think about it
Think about it
She said
Sex is not love
Love is not sex
Think about it
Think about it
You are not a devil's advocate
Because
You are not pragmatic enough
You will only go with
What everyone else says
And spit in my face
In the process
So if you want to
Treat me like a pig
Fine
Then I will
Treat you like a bitch
Think about it
Think about it
I am tired
Of giving people like you
The benefit of the doubt
When all you do

Is criticize me
The moment I have turned
I am tired
Of gripping people like you
When you affect me
Like an ingrown toe nail
Of which I have no problem
Removing myself
Without anaesthetic
You gave no forward
So I will give you no afterward
Think about it
Think about it
Earlier today
He said to me
"Keep my chin up"
But that's where
I keep on taking it
No matter if
It is up or down
Some things have to be settled
Some things will be settled
One way or another
I will make sure
That we are even
I have gotten mine
Sooner or later
You will get yours
Think about it
Think about it

#1024

SEEING THINGS

A few days ago
A female I work with
Called me a bad man
Yesterday she threw
An envelope full of photographs at me
Both unprovoked
If I had done the same
I would have been reprimanded
On Good Friday
All the girls stood in a group
Disrespecting men in their talk
And refusing to talk to me
If I do the same
About women
I am a pig

A few days ago
On the bus
A cute young raver girl got on
And the woman behind me
(Who was about 65)
Said the girl was stupid
Older people nowadays
Seem to have no respect
For younger people
And still expect to be respected
You can't get respect
From people when you disrespect them
You can't make friends with people
When you hurt these same people
I wish I was imagining these things
But I am seeing these things

#1181

AMERICAN WAR

This is the stink
Of the apple pie that you just puked up
This is the stink
Of what you thought you conquered
The sand and hot wind
That blows
Stings your already sunburnt flesh
Write home
When the next car bomb goes off asshole
Your most reliable news resources
Is a bunch of candy coated racists
And wouldn't dare interview
Ken Jarecke
From the last time around
You know what
There never will be
A world without tears
When a war on nothing
Gets better television ratings
Than the Superbowl and/or the World Series
Death is the way
The only way out
To be reprogrammed
Follow the cult's orders
And death for YOU is the way
The only way out
You started it
You started this war on nothing
And they will finish it
This American War

#812
OLD TIMERS

Bit by bit
I assault your senses
The more I write
The more I hope
It kills part of you
That is precious to you
Part of you that you never even knew existed
Why won't you
Remember my name
Can't find the light switch
Here
Let me get it for you
I will turn out the lights
And follow right behind you
Waiting for the moment
That you relax
It will come soon
Because no one
Expects anything like this
From me and my hands
Shut the hell up
You and your
Stupid mindless drivel
Is making me
Want to confine you
To a small room
With several large rats
That haven't eaten
In about week or two
It is about time
That you leave
I was getting sick
Of being
In the same room with you
And no I won't be offended
By you leaving
In fact I will rejoice
Because by you leaving
Means that there is

More room for
Younger people
With more innocent energy
To replace your
Stale bigotry
With something
More productive
If you can't keep up
Then drop out

#1149

APPRENTICESHIP

You ask me
To give something
That you gave to me
As a gift
To someone else

You told me
That I was wrong
That I was overly sensitive
Then you left me
Then you came back to me
Crying
Telling me that you were wrong
And I was right all along

You thought
I was sleeping
In the other room
When you told others
That you won't leave anything
In your will to me
Because I will never get married
I wasn't sleeping
In the other room
I heard it all

You all
Never gave me a chance
And never give me a chance
It is quite obvious
I am supposed to learn
From this
What I have learned is
To use call display
To have a long memory
To have a selective memory
And to use my work on you
Like the Al-Quada
Used jets on 9-11

The difference between
The Al-Quada and myself
Is that I will never go away to regroup
I don't need to
Because no matter how much you knock me down
My work keeps coming back
When I am down
In the bottom of the ninth

#1151

PAYBACK

What goes around
Comes around
Spare me the greetings
Because I don't get it
All the false smiles
And the sheepish words
When it all winds down
I know that I will win
I always do
It may take years
But I always laugh last
The hardest and last
Sometimes
When I am caught
At a weaker moment
I wonder if you can handle it
But then I remember
That disrespect is a two way street
And you have got
What's coming to you

ATHEISM INCORPORATED

#1155

I resent being treated
Like a cause to be championed
I don't need to be saved
By you and your kind

I have saved myself
And I have seen the future
It is the complete works
Of someone
Who has been fist fucked
By the likes of
You, your good book and your company

Of someone
Of me
I have saved myself
And you cannot stop me
From coming after you
Your good book and your company
With an ice pick
That is how much I resented
You and your kind

Would we be alive
Without your piss ass god

Yes

#831

Your tears
Won't put out
My fire
Because sometimes
I don't know
What to write
When most times
I write exactly
How I feel
Whether it hurts you
Or not

ASCETICAL

I need no alms
Because I am the Doppler effect
For real
Even from miles away
You can hear, see, taste
And even feel
Me coming closer
You can hear, see, taste
And even feel
My work coming closer
To you
The more you reject me
The stronger I get
The more you reject me
The stronger my work gets
I starve myself
And only live on my work
And off of your rejection

Subject: I received your mail
Date: Sat, 22 May 1999 01:41:16 -0600
From: █████████@worldgate.com>
To: ███████@dramaticsituations.com

Hi Corey:

I don't normally comment on web sites or unsolicited messages in my email . . . it must be the evening.

Your web site says more about you than your mail out. The letter carrier junkmail that you sent has that "recent graduate" feel to it that I don't believe defines you correctly and frankly, is detrimental to your professional image. Anyone who receives this in the ad/design, that normally only has 10 seconds for every piece of mail, would deliver it to file 13 quite rapidly (can yo say Michael Jordan.)

I have a biz address at home even though my co. has a different address. If I would have received this at the office, either my assistant or myself would have tossed it before it was actually read. My wife passed this to me in my home office tonight--this is the only reason I looked at your piece and went to your web site. Here's some personal insight that I think might help you for your next piece. Depending on your viewpoint, you will either believe I am soiling your Corn Flakes or asking you to step out of the box, (either is appropriate.)

In my opinion, you have wasted your money on the mail out. I get so much of this STUFF every week that I want to bring up the crappy food I eat at lunch every day! I constantly tell my designers, "if you make me feel uncomfortable, it's probably good." You didn't make me feel uncomfortable, hell, you made me feel tired. If you don't have the money to deliver something exceptional by post, then find another way.

Considering that your web site is a reasonably good representation of your work, perhaps a direct mail piece that encourages web use but doesn't "give away the farm" is a good idea. Think of it as a teaser campaign directed at building hits to your site. I believe that the things that you show for this "teaser," need to be so creative, outrageous, unconventional, and out-of-the-box, that your audience thinks of either burning them and saying 20 hail-marys or giving you a call and asking you to photograph, write, or design something. Make something that makes me or someone else want you (or at the very least hate you)!

And I guess, in my estimation, that's the crux of the matter. Will you bore me or my client audience? Those, who substantially remunerate me for delivering images and messages that demand attention? Do you have the creativity, the technical ability, and most importantly the vision to motivate me to actually take you for hire . . . you with no references . . . you without the "this guy's amazing" beer-after-golf kudos, you with the small, obligatory fill-the-space Edmonton Journal write-up?

Continued on the next page.

Make me want to rebel,
Make me want to take action,
Make me want to rise from my seat, put a stone through my monitor ar
tear the page before me,
Make me feel burning passion, searing anger, unbridled love or killi
hate,
Make me want to deliver death or life,
Make me think, then understand, and never forget,
This is the mark of a great designer.

Send me your next piece. I anticipate it.

L

I have seen your vision. You believe yourself different but you are p
of the masses.

1138 Frontenac Avenue SW
Calgary AB T2T 1B6
Tel:403-245-2491 Fax: 403-245-238C
▮frontenachouse.com
http://www.frontenachouse.com

Frontenac House Ltd.

July 30, 2004

Cory Hamilton
P.O. Box 696
Edmonton, AB
T5J 2L4

Dear Cory,

Thank you for submitting *No One Shall Be Spared* to us. It is a very well written and thought provoking work and I really enjoyed reading it. I'm sorry that in the end it was not among the manuscripts we chose for Quartet 2004. We had a great number of submissions this year and it was difficult selecting only four knowing that so many high quality collections would be rejected. Thanks again for submitting to us.

Best wishes,

Corey Hamilton was runner up in a grade 6 poetry recital contest. So there.

www.ingramcontent.com/pod-product-compliance
Lightning Source LLC
Chambersburg PA
CBHW050638300426
44112CB00012B/1850